Sidney Morgenbesser

Sidney Morgenbesser was born in New York City in 1921. He received a bachelor of science degree at The College of the City of New York in 1942. He has also attended The Jewish Theological Seminary of America and the University of Pennsylvania, from which he earned a doctorate in philosophy in 1955. Professor Morgenbesser has taught at Swarthmore College, The New School for Social Research, and Brandeis University, and is now Associate Professor of Philosophy at Columbia University. He has written several articles for professional philosophical journals, and is presently editor of the Journal of Philosophy. He is co-editor with Arthur Danto of *Philosophy of Science.*

James J. Walsh

James Walsh was born in Seattle, Washington, in 1924. He received a bachelor of arts degree from Reed College in 1949. As a Rhodes scholar, he attended Oxford University, earning a bachelor of arts degree in 1951, and a master of arts degree in 1956. He received a doctorate in philosophy from Columbia University in 1960. Dr. Walsh has taught at the University of California at Berkeley, and is presently Assistant Professor of Philosophy at Columbia University. He is author of *Aristotle's Conception of Akrasia,* to be published in 1962.

FREE WILL

FREE WILL

Edited by

SIDNEY MORGENBESSER

JAMES WALSH

A SPECTRUM BOOK

Prentice-Hall, Inc., *Englewood Cliffs, N. J.*

Contents

FREE WILL

Introduction

I

The free will problem can arise in several ways. In this brief introduction we want only to indicate some of these ways, without attempting anything like a resolution of the problem, and without supposing that all the concepts employed meet the standards of clarity which are common in contemporary philosophy. Hume seems to have supposed that the problem, the formulation of which, he claimed, is confused, would disappear with the proper analysis of its terms. Whether or not this sanguine expectation is well-founded, there is no doubt that many of the central concepts of the problem could stand analysis and that much progress could thus be made with the issue. But this is not our concern here. We should also like to point out a peculiarity of the problem which Mabbott once noticed: that whereas Determinist positions are very often elaborately developed, Libertarian positions tend to be polemical in statement, concentrating on the refutation of Determinist claims. The Libertarian often finds it difficult to say positively what it is that he intends. This need not imply that what he intends is not of great philosophical importance.

One of the most obvious ways the problem can come up is in the worry about Fate. There are many inevitabilities in human life, and it is a common practice to generalize this idea. *Che sera, sera* is sometimes a useful phrase, enabling one to shrug off minor worries; but it can lead to very great worry indeed: does a man *ever* control his own destiny, will all things turn out as they will no matter *what* he does? The idea that there is a Fate, some necessary way that things must be, has occasionally seized the imagination of whole cultures—as can be seen in many writings of the Greeks. Sometimes there is no *ground* for such a belief in Fate—the worry is, as it were, philosophically pure. But sometimes the belief in Fate is an outgrowth of some further belief, such as in the omnipotence of God. If God created the world, He must have created it down to the most minute detail, and if He is its ruler, nothing must escape His constant control. We then have the idea that men are the

1

puppets of God. There have been other grounds for the worry about
Fate, one of the most unusual of which involves the logical principle
that every proposition must be either true or false and not both. The
principle surely must also apply to propositions which describe future
happenings. If such propositions must already be determinate with regard to truth or falsity, does not this imply that the happenings themselves must be predetermined in some way? Philosophers have spent
considerable energy exorcising the bogey of Fate in all its forms, and in
so doing, have been led to consider at least some aspects of the free will
problem.

Now let us turn to one of the most philosophically interesting ap-
proaches to the problem, the approach through the concepts of reason
and action. One of the problems that has most interested philosophers
is: what is it that uniquely distinguishes man from the rest of nature?
There are obviously many things that only man does: only man reads
newspapers, only man wears cosmetics, only man laughs; but philosophers
have often thought that there is one human faculty which is the precondition for any of these others. They have often called this Reason.
What, then, is this Reason which is the *sine qua non* for all other
uniquely human activities? The term "Reason" covers in its turn any
number of activities and processes: using language, interpreting percep-
tions, perhaps intuiting certain special types of truths, and so on. There
are two of these processes which are related and which, when closely considered, can lead to aspects of the free will problem. One is what we
sometimes call "reasoning"—considering premisses and coming to a conclusion. Some philosophers have thought that some kind of causal account might be given of this process of reasoning. Hume, for instance,
remarked that reason is and ought to be the slave of the passions, which
would imply that reasoning can only occur under the stimulus of passion. This still leaves open the question of what might be called the
proper features of reasoning; or belief in the premiss and inference from
premiss to conclusion. But here again Hume offers a causal account, reducing belief to vivacity of image and inference to association. Not
many would agree with the details of Hume's theory, but he has raised
the general question as to whether there can be a causal theory of reasoning, or whether to attempt such a theory involves some fundamental
philosophical mistake.

The second process, deliberation, is one kind of reasoning that raises
other problems even more directly involving the free will problem. Deliberation we will take quite simply as reasoning about what to do. It seems
a safe enough assumption that this process of deliberation has no point
unless the situation confronting the deliberator is in some sense "open"
—that is, unless there are genuine alternative possibilities. What, then,
are we to make of this notion of "genuine possibilities?" Philosophers
can be bothered on two scores when confronted with this notion. Some

believe that there are no contingencies in nature because everything that happens has a necessitating cause. Others believe that everything which exists is a concrete actuality, and that the notion of a "possibility" is an abstract idea which should be eliminated. On either ground, deliberation remains a problem.

The conclusion of deliberation is usually called decision, and here we encounter further difficulties. For some philosophers have urged that it makes no sense for a person to predict his *own* decisions. They have claimed that for a person to predict that he will make a certain decision is really for him to announce his decision in advance—that is, to *make* the decision in its prediction. Does this imply that decisions are essentially unpredictable? Presumably psychologists and social scientists often predict the decisions of others; why then should a decision be predictable by someone else and not by the one who reaches it? This may be a mere conundrum, but there are other difficulties associated with the concept of decision which are of a more serious nature. The concept of decision is the concept of a practically *effective* conclusion to deliberation, and thus may be merely a cover for a philosphical problem. Some philosophers have wondered how deliberation can *be* practically effective—that is, how a *mental* process can be related to a *physical* process such as the movement of the body which is involved in human actions. Some have supposed that there is a kind of intervening process, which they have called "volition." The full concept of decision, then, would be that of a mental conclusion to deliberation which sets off a volition which in turn sets off an appropriate movement of the body. In this way a criterion can be developed for distinguishing between human *actions* and mere bodily *movements*. An action will be a movement which includes a volition in its causes. Needless to say, such an account meets with small favor among many philosophers, who point out that no such criterion is employed in our common understanding of actions, and who object to the systematic elusiveness of such volitions when it comes to empirical verification. But once again, an objectionable theory points to a real problem. It may be true that we do not ordinarily search for any such mysterious process as volition in discovering whether a person *did* something or whether what happened was merely a physical movement; but we still do employ a distinction between doing something intentionally and not doing something at all, and we would elaborate on the notion of doing something intentionally by saying that the person knew what he was doing and often, had decided to do it. What *is* the difference, then, between mere physical movement and intentional action?

We are thus brought to another way in which the free will problem can arise—and this is perhaps by far the most common way. It is by reflection upon the conditions for moral responsibility and the possible incompatibilities of those conditions with the determination of human actions that philosophers (and not only philosophers) have been led to wonder whether men have free will, and if they do, what this free will might be. Let us start by asking what men are considered to be morally responsible for. The answer is that they are held responsible for many things—for actions, obviously, but also for failures to act, for carelessness, for some kinds of ignorance, and so on. To explore all the possibilities here would be an extremely extended undertaking, so let us concentrate only on the most obvious candidates for responsibility, actions. Is a man, then, responsible for *all* his actions—that is, is he responsible for *everything* he does? We are accustomed to say that he is *only* responsible for some actions, and we often make the distinction by saying that it is only for the ones he does freely, or of his own free will, or voluntarily, that he is held responsible; he is not held responsible for what he does involuntarily. Some care should be taken in proceeding from this distinction, for the notion of a voluntary act can have more than one sense. In one sense, an act is voluntary as opposed to constrained. We might say that a man who gave his money to a thief rather than lose his life was constrained or forced to give up the money. But in another sense, an act is voluntary as opposed to being involuntary. Thus a man who sneezes is said to have acted involuntarily. Long ago, philosophers noted that both voluntary and involuntary actions in the *first* sense are voluntary in the *second* sense, and they exploited this by saying that there can be no coercion of a will—which simply means that the man who gave up his money *could* have chosen to lose his life instead, as he might if honor had meant more to him than prosperity. Another thing to note here is that we might want to say that a so-called "involuntary action" is not an action at all, for performances like sneezing are not something that a man *does*. We could formulate this important distinction in two ways, then: either as the distinction between voluntary and involuntary action, or as the distinction between action and, let us say, mere behavior. Then we must ask what is the difference, however we formulate it. The obvious answer is that the sneeze was not in the person's power, that it was not up to him whether he sneezed or not, that it was caused by something over which he had no control. And now we come to a problem, for some thinkers have held that *all* actions are caused. If this were true, would it place *all* actions in the same class with the sneeze, and thus obliterate the distinction between voluntary and involuntary action?

There are various sorts of doctrines regarding the causation of human actions. One kind of doctrine merely asserts that actions are predictable on the basis of statistical generalizations, and this we will set to one side as being compatible with the distinction between voluntary and involuntary action. Another kind includes specific causal theories, ranging from crude theories based on the egotism of human desires to much more sophisticated theories based on laws of learning or the physics of the brain. It is the merit of these specific theories that they are subject to empirical tests; and again we will set them to one side, at least for the moment, as being philosophically straightforward. A third kind of doctrine is much more general. It asserts that regardless of the failure of this or that specific theory, *some* causal theory of human action is in principle possible, on the ground that it is a metaphysical truth that every event must have a cause, or on the more circumspect ground that causal theories have been developed for all other items in nature and there is no reason for excluding human action from the progress of natural science. Some philosophers have supposed that if such a doctrine were true, it would still not be the case that all actions must be assimilated to the sneeze, because they hold that an action can have a cause without being *totally* determined by that cause. Other philosophers would say that this kind of a doctrine makes nonsense of the concept of causation.

The concept of causation is itself far from clear, and once again, rather than trace through the complexities of what amounts in itself to a major philosophical inquiry, we will concentrate on a fairly obvious and neutral version: that of acting under conditions. In order to do justice to the bearing of all this on the free will problem, we will further distinguish between necessary and sufficient conditions. Now let us see what light this distinction will shed on the differences between Determinists, who would hold that actions have causes, and Libertarians, who would deny this.

Some Libertarians, such as Descartes, have said that the free will is infinite in some sense, and this might be interpreted to mean that men can do anything under any conditions. But even Descartes would distinguish between divine omnipotence and human free will and admit the obvious fact that for many actions there are necessary conditions. A man cannot solve difficult equations if he is very stupid, nor can he finish a race if he is exhausted. To deny this would suggest that stupidity and exhaustion are conditions a person somehow chooses to have. Sartre seems to say something like this, but few Libertarians would go so far. We have, then, the innocuous position that for *some* actions there are necessary conditions. Then the question arises, are there necessary conditions for *all* actions? Libertarians might want to make two distinctions before answering the question. The first is the distinction between trivial and non-trivial necessary conditions. They might point out that there are some conditions which are necessary for all actions, only in the sense that they are necessary for both the performance of an action and for its opposite. Thus, if a man sees someone drowning, he can either dive in and swim after him or turn and walk away. In either case he must have a body, be alive, and so forth. The second is the distinction between ordinary and recondite actions. Thus a man may not finish a race when exhausted, but perhaps he can *make an effort* to finish even when exhausted, or perhaps he can at least *refuse to give in* even if he cannot manage a real effort. St. Augustine, for instance, seems to have thought that one could give or withold his consent under *any* conditions. The Libertarian position would be, then, that there are certain privileged actions, perhaps of this recondite type, for which there are at most trivially necessary conditions, and for which there are no necessary conditions which are peculiar to the actions. It may be true that for a will to be free it must be present and intact, but when present and intact, it is not subject to any conditions for its essential act. For instance, if the privileged action is that of refusing to give in, then it is not required that the runner have a desire to finish the race in order to carry through this refusal, even though there may come a point when exhaustion overwhelms him and he can no longer either give in or refuse to do so. There is a certain danger in this position which should be noted, for as such necessary conditions are found for the more obvious kinds of action, a systematic retreat to more and more recondite kinds can be carried on. It may then be difficult to say whether such a retreat expresses deeper and deeper insight into the recesses of the will or merely a resolution to prolong the controversy no matter what the evidence may be.

Other Libertarians would brush aside these subtleties and admit that there may be non-trivial necessary conditions for all kinds of action. But they would deny that there must be *sufficient* conditions for all kinds of actions. Why should the line be drawn here? The answer is very simple to say, but not so simple to understand. It is that if there *are* sufficient conditions—or, what would be even stronger, necessary and sufficient conditions, then no one could ever act otherwise than he does. And if no one can act otherwise than he does, then no one ever has any choice in what he does. If no one ever has any choice, then no one is ever morally responsible. This leaves us with two questions which are crucial to the free will problem: for a man to be morally responsible, *must* he be able to act otherwise than he does; and, if we say that a man *is* able to act otherwise than he does, is this inconsistent with saying that there are sufficient conditions for his actions? Let us briefly consider why opposing answers have been given to both these questions.

For a man to be morally responsible, must he be able to act otherwise than he does? Many philosophers have answered "no" to this question, saying that all that is required for a person to be responsible for an action is that the sufficient conditions *include* his own wishes, desires, etc. Very often such a position goes along with a theory of punishment as merely reformative or deterrent. Other philosophers have answered "yes" to the question, on the ground that it is not enough for the person's wishes to be included in the conditions of action, since this leaves open the all-important possibility that the person has no control over his own wishes, and thus, over his own actions. Very often this position goes along with a theory of punishment as retributive, as giving a person "what he deserves" for what he does.

Even if we say that a man must be able to act otherwise than he does, is this at all inconsistent with there being sufficient conditions for his actions? Again, some philosophers have answered "no," and have urged that all that we mean when we say that a man could have acted otherwise than he does is that he *would* have acted otherwise *if* conditions had been different. To say that the runner *could* have made a greater effort than he did is to say, for instance, that he *would* have made that effort *if* he had cared more about finishing the race. Other philosophers find this a misleading analysis. It has a certain plausibility in the case of the exhausted runner, for there we are not sure whether we are talking about his ability to carry on or about his ability to *exercise* that ability *at will*. These philosophers hold that we may mean different things when we say that a person *can* do something, and that what we mean when we say that a person can act otherwise than he does *in the sense* in which this is required to hold a person responsible for what he does is *not* that he would act differently than he does under different conditions. The "can" in the case of moral agency is not hypothetical, but categorical.

It has been estimated that more has been written about free will than about any other philosophical problem. We do not pretend to have covered the field. But we hope enough has been done to indicate the basic aspects and to serve as a rough guide to the selections which follow.

II

It would be impossible to present a complete survey of positions concerning free will in an anthology of this size. Still, rather than to confine the selections to some very limited point of view, we have aimed at a representative sampling. This policy has placed a premium on wide-ranging discussions; the inclusion of a selection here does not at all imply that it is the most highly developed statement of its type. Certain important statements have been omitted because they are so readily available: there is little need to print once again selections from Plato, Descartes, Spinoza, Hume, Kant, or James. This also holds true for certain recent discussions such as those of Campbell, Nowell-Smith, and Austin, which have done a great deal to stimulate interest in the subject. We have also found that to exerpt from book-length treatments such as those offered by Hartmann and Farrer does not do justice to the course of their extended arguments. It is hoped that the bibliography at the end of the readings will compensate to some extent for these and many other omissions.

I

Background

The selections in this section are included as samples of four classic and historically important discussions of the problem of free will. We have respected the common view, here presented by Hobbes, that it is with Christian thinkers and especially with St. Augustine that the problem emerges, even though the various ingredients of his thought are to be found in previous thinkers. It is interesting that both Determinists and Libertarians claim St. Augustine as their ancestor, as is evidenced here by the fact that both Hobbes and Bramhall invoke his authority. Libertarians tend to appeal to his earlier writings, represented here by a selection from the treatise *On Free Will*, and Determinists tend to appeal to the later writings produced during his controversy with Pelagius, represented here by a selection from *The Spirit and the Letter*. Pelagius, a British heretic, urged men on to greater moral efforts by instilling in them a heightened sense of personal responsibility. This involved reducing original sin to the bad example of Adam, and the saving grace of Christ to His good example. Against this St. Augustine insisted that grace does not merely alter the circumstances of the will, but the will itself. God does not reward man's efforts—He makes those very efforts possible. It has seemed to many that St. Augustine shifted from his earlier insistence on the reality of free will to a strict theological determinism. He himself denied this, and there is in the second selection the distinction which has been much emphasized as the key to his consistency. This is the distinction between free will (*liberum arbitrium*), which belongs to man by nature and which he can never lose, and freedom (*libertas*), the ability to make good *use* of free will. It is freedom which is lost with original sin and recovered with grace. What sense can be made of free will without freedom is a problem discussed by followers of St. Augustine such as St. Anselm and the theologians of the Reformation.

St. Thomas Aquinas stands here as the representative of the Greek intellectualism which St. Augustine is considered by many to have repudiated and which is represented in later philosophy by Spinoza and perhaps by Kant. This is the doctrine that free will is based upon the freedom of the intellect, or, as St. Thomas puts it, free choice is free judgment. Other passages might be found in St. Thomas' writings which would balance this emphasis in the Augustinian direction. St. Thomas believes that the will is necessarily oriented to beatitude as its ultimate end, and it should be noticed that in trying to avoid a denial of free will, he distinguishes between coercive necessity, which is inconsistent with free will, and what he calls absolute and teleological necessity, which are not. This suggests the distinction between compulsion and causation on which Hume was to rest his case and which has been repeated by many philosophers who, like St. Thomas, wish to find in balanced views and judicious compromise the answer to the problem.

Duns Scotus is here as the great historical Libertarian. In the question from which this selection is taken he argues against two positions that would, in his eyes, endanger the freedom of the will. The first is that it is the object as it is *perceived* which is the effective cause of willing. (We have omitted most of this discussion, except for the bit which says that it is freedom rather than appetite which defines the will.) The second position is that it is the object as it is *known* which is the effective cause of willing. The tradition against which he argues here is often considered to include St. Thomas. For Duns Scotus, the freedom of the will is not due to its participation in the intellect, but rather, if freedom pertains to the intellect at all, it is because of its subjection to the will. That is, it is not because man deliberates that he is free, but because he can accept or reject the results of his deliberation at will. What we have here, though only a fragment, is central to his elaborate and thorough exploration of the problems which are raised by this position.

The reaction of the medievals to the views of Duns Scotus and his followers was prompt. A cry arose against the new Pelagians and a controversy developed which carried on into the sixteenth century and numbered Erasmus and Luther among its protagonists. What we find in the debate between Hobbes and Bramhall is on the one hand a continuation of this long and bitter struggle, and on the other, the suggestion of a newer version of the problem. In this newer version it is the fact that the human body is subject to the laws of motion rather than the fact that human actions are subject to the will of God which threatens the freedom of the will. Bramhall was Bishop of Derry, and is identified in the selection as J. D.; Hobbes, of course, is T. H. It was the virtue of seventeenth-century thinkers to write clearly, so we shall let the selection speak for itself. But it should be pointed out that Hobbes stands here at the beginning of a long British tradition including Locke, Hume, Mill and Nowell-Smith. Hobbes enunciates the principle of this tradition: that free will is consistent with determinism since it does not imply the freedom of something called the "will" from causal determination, but rather the freedom of the man from compulsion. The reader might also do well to notice that while Duns Scotus interprets contingency as a property of events, Hobbes interprets it as the uncertainty of our knowledge.

From *On Free Will*

ST. AUGUSTINE

BOOK III

Evodius.—It is sufficiently evident to me that free will is to be numbered among the good things, and, indeed, not among the least of our good things. We are, therefore, compelled to confess that it has been given us by God, and that he has rightly given it to us. But now, if you think a suitable time has come, I want to learn from you whence arises the movement by which the will itself turns from the unchangeable good, which is the common property of all, to its own interests or to the interests of others or to things beneath it, and so turns to mutable goods. *Augustine.*—Why must you know this? *Evodius.*—Because if free will is so given that it has that movement by nature, it turns of necessity to mutable goods; and no blame attaches where nature and necessity prevail. *Augustine.*—Do you like or dislike that movement? *Evodius.*—I dislike it. *Augustine.*—So you find fault with it? *Evodius.*—I do. *Augustine.*—Then you find fault with a movement of the mind though it is faultless. *Evodius.*—No, I do not. But I do not know whethere there is any fault in abandoning the unchangeable good and turning towards the mutable goods. *Augustine.*—Then you are finding fault with something which you do not know. *Evodius.*—Don't insist on a verbal point. I said that I did not know whether there was any fault, but I meant to be understood really as having no doubt about it. Certainly I said I do not know, but obviously I was being ironical in suggesting that there could be any doubt about so clear a matter. *Augustine.*—Just consider what is that truth you hold to be so certain that it has caused you so soon to forget what you said a moment ago. If that movement of the will exists by nature or necessity, it is in no way culpable. And yet you are so firmly convinced that it is culpable that you think fit to wax ironical about hesitation over

From *On Free Will* (De Libero Arbitrio), i, 1-3; ii, 4-5; iii, 6-8; iv, 9-11. Printed in *Augustine, Earlier Writings,* selected and translated with introductions by J. H. S. Burleigh. "The Library of Christian Classics," Vol. VI (Philadelphia: The Westminster Press, 1955). Reprinted by permission.

a matter so certain. Why did you think it right to affirm, or at least to say with some hesitation, what you yourself show to be obviously false? You said: "If free will has been given in such fashion that it has that movement by nature, then it turns to mutable things of necessity, and no fault can be found where nature and necessity rule." But you ought to have had no doubt that it was not given in that fashion, since you do not doubt that that movement is culpable. *Evodius.*—I said that the movement is culpable, and that therefore it displeases me, and that I cannot doubt that it is reprehensible. But I hold that a soul which is thereby drawn from the unchangeable good to mutable goods is not to be blamed if its nature is such that it is so moved by necessity.

Augustine.—To whom belongs the movement which you admit is blameworthy? *Evodius.*—I see that it is in the soul, but to whom it belongs I know not. *Augustine.*—You do not deny that the soul is moved by that motion? *Evodius.*—No. *Augustine.*—Do you then deny that the motion by which a stone is moved is the motion of the stone? I don't mean the motion that we give to it, or that is given to it by some other force, when it is thrown upwards, but that by which of its own accord it falls back to earth. *Evodius.*—I do not deny that the motion you refer to, by which it turns and falls downwards, is the motion of the stone, but it is its natural motion. If the motion of the soul is like that, it too is natural, and it cannot rightly be blamed for a motion that is natural. Even if it moves to its own destruction, it is compelled by the necessity of its own nature. Moreover because we have no doubt that the soul's motion is culpable we must absolutely deny that it is natural, and therefore not like the motion of the stone, which is natural motion. *Augustine.*—Did we achieve anything in our two previous discussions? *Evodius.*—I am sure we did. *Augustine.*—No doubt you remember that in the first discussion we discovered that the mind can become the slave of lust only by its own will. No superior thing and no equal thing compels it to such dishonor, because that would be unjust. And no inferior thing has the power. It remains that that must be the mind's own motion when it turns its will away from enjoyment of the Creator to enjoyment of the creature. If that motion is accounted blameworthy—and you thought anyone who doubted that deserved to be treated ironically—it is not natural but voluntary. It is like the motion of the falling stone, in so far as it is a motion of the soul as the former is the motion of the stone. But it is dissimilar in this, that it is not in the power of a stone to arrest its downward motion, while if the soul is not willing it cannot be moved to abandon what is higher and to love what is lower. Thus the stone's motion is natural, the soul's voluntary. Hence anyone who says that a stone sins when it is carried downwards by its own weight is, I will not say more senseless than the stone but, completely mad. But we charge the soul with sin when we show that it has abandoned the higher things and prefers to enjoy lower things. What need is there, therefore, to seek the origin of the movement whereby the will turns from the unchangeable to the changeable good? We acknowledge that it is a movement of the soul, that it is voluntary and therefore culpable. And all useful learning in this matter has its object and value in teaching us to condemn and restrain that movement, and to convert our wills from falling into temporal delights to the enjoyment of the eternal good.

Evodius.—I see, and in a sense grasp that what you say is true. There is nothing that I feel more certainly and more personally than that I have a will, and that it moves me to enjoy this or that. I know nothing I could call my own if the will by which I will "yea" or "nay" is not my own. If I use it to do evil, to whom is the evil to be attributed if not to myself? Since a good God has made me, and I can do nothing right except by willing, it is clearly evident that it was to this end that the will has been given to me by God who is good. Moreover, unless the movement of the will towards this or that object is voluntary and within our power, a man would not be praiseworthy when he turns to the higher objects nor blameworthy when he turns to lower objects, using his will like a hinge. There would be no use at all in warning him to pay no attention to temporal things and to will to obtain the eternal things, or to will to live aright and to be unwilling to live an evil life. But whoever thinks that man is not to be so warned ought to be cut off from membership in the human race.

That being so, I have a deep desire to know how it can be that God knows all things beforehand and that, nevertheless, we do not sin by necessity. Whoever says that anything can happen otherwise than as God has foreknown it, is attempting to destroy the divine foreknowledge with the most insensate impiety. If God foreknew that the first man would sin—and that anyone must concede who acknowledges with me that God has foreknowledge of all future events—I do not say that God did not make him, for he made him good, nor that the sin of the creature whom he made good could be prejudicial to God. On the contrary, God showed his goodness in making man, his justice in punishing his sin, and his mercy in delivering him. I do not say, therefore, that God did not make man. But this I say. Since God foreknew that man would sin, that which God foreknew must necessarily come to pass. How then is the will free when there is apparently this unavoidable necessity?

Augustine.—You have knocked vigorously. May God in his mercy grant us his presence and open the door to those who knock. But I verily believe that the vast majority of men are troubled by that question for no other reason than that they do not ask it in a pious fashion. They are swifter to make excuses for their sins than to make confession of them. Some are glad to hold the opinion that there is no divine providence presiding over human affairs. They commit themselves, body and soul, to fortuitous circumstances, and deliver themselves to be carried about and tormented by lusts. They deny that there is any divine judgment, and deceive human judges when they are accused. They imagine that they are driven on by the favor of fortune. In sculpture or painting they are wont to represent Fortune as blind, either because they are better than the goddess by whom they think they are ruled, or because they confess that in their sentiments they are afflicted with that same blindness. In the case of such people it is not absurd to admit that they do everything by chance, seeing that they stumble in all that they do. But against this opinion, so full of foolish and senseless error, we have, I think, sufficiently spoken in our second disputation. Others do not venture to deny that the providence of God presides over human affairs, but they would rather indulge in the wicked error of believing that providence is weak or unjust or evil than confess their sins with suppliant piety. If all these would suffer themselves to be persuaded to believe that the goodness, justice and power of God are greater far, and far superior to any thought they can have of goodness, justice or might, if they would but take thought to themselves, they would know that they owe thanks to God, even if he had willed them to be somewhat lower in the scale of being than they actually are, and with all that is within them they would exclaim with the Psalmist: "I have spoken: Lord have mercy upon me; heal my soul for I have sinned against thee" (Ps. 41:5). So by stages the divine mercy would bring them to wisdom. They would be neither inflated by what they discover, nor rebellious when they fail to find the truth; by learning they would become better prepared to see the truth, and by recognizing their ignorance they would become more patient in seeking it. I am quite sure that these are your views too. Now first answer a few questions I am going to put to you, and you will see how easily I can find a solution to your tremendous problem.

Your trouble is this. You wonder how it can be that these two propositions are not contradictory and incompatible, namely that God has foreknowledge of all future events, and that we sin voluntarily and not by necessity. For if, you say, God foreknows that a man will sin, he must necessarily sin. But if there is necessity there is no voluntary choice in sinning, but rather fixed and unavoidable necessity. You are afraid that by that reasoning the conclusion may be reached either that God's foreknowledge of all future events must be impiously denied, or, if that cannot be denied, that sin is committed not voluntarily but by necessity. Isn't that your difficulty? *Evodius.*—Exactly that. *Augustine.*—You think, therefore, that all things of which God has foreknowledge happen by necessity and not voluntarily. *Evodius.*—Yes. Absolutely. *Augustine.*— Try an experiment, and examine yourself a little, and tell me what kind of will you are going to have to-morrow. Will you want to sin or to do right? *Evodius.*—I do not know. *Augustine.*—Do you think God also does not know? *Evodius.*—I could in no wise think that. *Augustine.*—If God knows what you are going to will tomorrow, and foresees what all men are going to will in the future, not only those who are at present alive but all who will ever be, much more will he foresee what he is going to do with the just and the impious? *Evodius.*—Certainly if I say that God has foreknowledge of my deeds, I should say with even greater confidence that he has foreknowledge of his own acts, and foresees with complete certainty what he is going to do. *Augustine.*—Don't you see that you will have to be careful lest someone say to you that, if all things of which God has foreknowledge are done by necessity and not voluntarily, his own future acts will be done not voluntarily but by necessity? *Evodius.*— When I said that all future events of which God has foreknowledge happen by necessity, I was having regard only to things which happen within his creation, and not to things which happen in God himself. Indeed, in God nothing happens. Everything is eternal. *Augustine.*— God, then, is not active within his creation? *Evodius.*—He determined once for all how the order of the universe he created was to go on, and he never changes his mind. *Augustine.*—Does he never make anyone happy? *Evodius.*—Indeed he does. *Augustine.*—He does it precisely at the time when the man in question actually becomes happy. *Evodius.*— That is so. *Augustine.*—If, then, for example, you yourself are happy one year from now, you will be made happy at that time. *Evodius.*— Exactly. *Augustine.*—God knows to-day what he is going to do a year hence? *Evodius.*—He eternally had that foreknowledge, but I agree that he has it now, if indeed it is to happen so.

Augustine.—Now tell me, are you not God's creature? And will not your becoming happy take place within your experience? *Evodius.*— Certainly I am God's creature, and if I become happy it will be within my experience. *Augustine.*—If God, then, makes you happy, your happiness will come by necessity and not by the exercise of your will? *Evodius.*—God's will is my necessity. *Augustine.*—Will you then be happy against your will? *Evodius.*—If I had the power to be happy, I should be so at once. For I wish to be happy but am not, because not I but God makes me happy. *Augustine.*—The truth simply cries out against you. You could not imagine that "having in our power" means anything else than "being able to do what we will." Therefore there is nothing so much in our power as is the will itself. For as soon as we will [*volumus*] immediately will [*voluntas*] is there. We can say rightly that we do not grow old voluntarily but necessarily, or that we do not die voluntarily but from necessity, and so with other similar things. But who but a raving fool would say that it is not voluntarily that we will? Therefore though God knows how we are going to will in the future, it is not proved that we do not voluntarily will anything. When you said that you did not make yourself happy, you said it as if I had denied it. What I say is that when you become happy in the future it will take place not against your will but in accordance with your willing. Therefore, though God has foreknowledge of your happiness in the future, and though nothing can happen otherwise than as he has foreknown it (for that would mean that there is no foreknowledge) we are not thereby compelled to think that you will not be happy voluntarily. That would be absurd and far from true. God's foreknowledge, which is even to-day quite certain that you are to be happy at a future date, does not rob you of your will to happiness when you actually attain happiness. Similarly if ever in the future you have a culpable will, it will be none the less your will because God had foreknowledge of it.

Observe, pray, how blind are those who say that if God has foreknowledge of what I am going to will, since nothing can happen otherwise than as he has foreknown it, therefore I must necessarily will what he has foreknown. If so, it must be admitted that I will, not voluntarily but from necessity. Strange folly! Is there, then, no difference between things that happen according to God's foreknowledge where there is no intervention of man's will at all, and things that happen because of a will of which he has foreknowledge? I omit the equally monstrous assertion of the man I mentioned a moment ago, who says I must necessarily so will. By assuming necessity he strives to do away with will altogether. If I must necessarily will, why need I speak of willing at all? But if he puts it in another way, and says that, because he must necessarily so will, his will is not in his own power, he can be countered by the answer you gave me when I asked whether you could become happy against your will. You replied that you would be happy now if the matter were in your power, for you willed to be happy but could not achieve it. And I added that the truth cries out against you; for we cannot say we do not have the power unless we do not have what we will. If we do not have the will, we may think we will but in fact we do not. If we cannot will without willing, those who will have will, and all that is in our power we have by willing. Our will would not be will unless it were in our power. Because it is in our power, it is free. We have nothing that is free which is not in our power, and if we have something it cannot be nothing. Hence it is not necessary to deny that God has foreknowledge of all things, while at the same time our wills are our own. God has foreknowledge of our will, so that of which he has foreknowledge must come to pass. In other words, we shall exercise our wills in the future because he has foreknowledge that we shall do so; and there can be no will or voluntary action unless it be in our power. Hence God has also foreknowledge of our power to will. My power is not taken from me by God's foreknowledge. Indeed I shall be more certainly in possession of my power because he whose foreknowledge is never mistaken, foreknows that I shall have the power. *Evodius.*—Now I no longer deny that whatever God has foreknown must necessarily come to pass, nor that he has foreknowledge of our sins, but in such a way that our wills remain free and within our power.

Augustine.—What further difficulty do you have? Perhaps you have forgotten what we established in our first disputation, and now wish to deny that we sin voluntarily and under no compulsion from anything superior, inferior or equal to us. *Evodius.*—I do not venture to deny that at all. But I must confess I do not yet see how God's foreknowledge of our sins and our freedom of will in sinning can be other than mutually contradictory. We must confess that God is just and knows all things beforehand. But I should like to know with what justice he punishes sins which must necessarily be committed; or how they are not necessarily committed when he knows that they will be committed; or how the Creator is to escape having imputed to him anything that happens necessarily in his creature.

Augustine.—Why do you think our free will is opposed to God's foreknowledge? Is it because it is foreknowledge simply, or because it is God's foreknowledge? *Evodius.*—In the main because it is God's foreknowledge. *Augustine.*—If you knew in advance that such and such a man would sin, there would be no necessity for him to sin. *Evodius.*—Indeed there would, for I should have no real foreknowledge unless I knew for certain what was going to happen. *Augustine.*—So it is foreknowledge generally and not God's foreknowledge specially that causes the events foreknown to happen by necessity? There would be no such thing as foreknowledge unless there was certain foreknowledge. *Evodius.*—I agree. But why these questions? *Augustine.*—Unless I am mistaken, you would not directly compel the man to sin, though you knew beforehand that he was going to sin. Nor does your prescience in itself compel him to sin even though he was certainly going to sin, as we must assume if you have real prescience. So there is no contradiction here. Simply you know beforehand what another is going to do with his own will. Similarly God compels no man to sin, though he sees beforehand those who are going to sin by their own will.

Why then should he not justly punish sins which, though he had foreknowledge of them, he did not compel the sinner to commit? Just as you apply no compulsion to past events by having them in your memory, so God by his foreknowledge does not use compulsion in the case of future events. Just as you remember your past actions, though all that you remember were not actions of your own, so God has foreknowledge of all his own actions, but is not the agent of all that he foreknows. Of evil actions he is not the agent but the just punisher. From this you may understand with what justice God punishes sins, for he has no responsibility for the future actions of men though he knows them beforehand. If he ought not to award punishment to sinners because he knew beforehand that they would sin, he ought not to reward the righteous, because he knew equally that they would be righteous. Let us confess that it belongs to his foreknowledge to allow no future event to escape his knowledge, and that it belongs to his justice to see that no sin goes unpunished by his judgment. For sin is committed voluntarily and not by any compulsion from his foreknowledge.

From *The Spirit and the Letter*

ST. AUGUSTINE

Do we then "make void" freedom of choice through grace? "God forbid! yea, we establish" freedom of choice. As the law is not made void by faith, so freedom of choice is not made void but established by grace. Freedom of choice is necessary to the fulfilment of the law. But by the law comes the knowledge of sin; by faith comes the obtaining of grace against sin; by grace comes the healing of the soul from sin's sickness; by the healing of the soul comes freedom of choice; by freedom of choice comes the love of righteousness; by the love of righteousness comes the working of the law. And thus, as the law is not made void but established by faith, since faith obtains the grace whereby the law may be fulfilled, so freedom of choice is not made void but established by grace, since grace heals the will whereby righteousness may freely be loved. All the links in that chain which I have drawn out are found speaking in the Holy Scriptures. The law says, "Thou shalt not covet." Faith says, "Heal my soul, for I have sinned against thee." Grace says, "Behold, thou art made whole: sin no more, lest a worse thing come unto thee." Health restored says, "O Lord my God, I cried unto thee and thou hast healed me." Freedom of choice says, "I will sacrifice freely unto thee." Love of righteousness says, "The unrighteous have spoken unto me of delights, but not as thy law, O Lord." Why then must wretched men be bold to vaunt themselves either of their freedom of choice before they are made free, or of their own strength, if the freedom has been given them? Why will they not hear in the very words "freedom of choice" the meaning of liberty? "Where the Spirit of the Lord is, there is liberty." How, if they are slaves of sin, can they boast freedom of choice? "For of whom a man is overcome, to the same is he brought in bondage." But if they have been made free, why boast of it as though it were their own work, and glory as though they had not received it? This is a freedom which will not have even him for master who says: "Without me ye can do nothing," and "If the Son shall make you free, then shall ye be free indeed."

From *The Spirit and the Letter*, articles 52-58, printed in *Augustine: Later Works*, selected and translated with introductions by John Burnaby. "The Library of Christian Classics," Vol. VIII (Philadelphia: The Westminster Press, 1955). Reprinted by permission.

In this linked series which I have described, the beginning of salvation
or of the way to it appears to be faith. The question will be asked, Is
this faith itself placed in our own power? It will help us to see the answer,
if we look somewhat more attentively into the nature of power. Willing
is one thing, ability another; willing does not necessarily imply ability,
nor ability willing: we sometimes will what we are not able to do, and
sometimes are able to do what we do not will. The Latin words make it
plain that will (*voluntas*) is derived from *velle,* power (*potestas*) from
posse: he who wills has *voluntas,* he who is able has *potestas.* But will
must be present for power to be operative: we do not call an unwilling
act the operation of power. Yet on a closer analysis, it appears that even
if you do a thing under compulsion, unwillingly, you do it by your will
if you do it at all: you are said to do it against your will, that is, unwillingly, because you would prefer to act differently. You are compelled to
act because of some evil, which it is your will to avoid or remove; and
so you act under compulsion. If your will were strong enough to prefer
the suffering of the evil to the doing of the act, you would of course resist
the compulsion and refuse the act. Thus if you act, though it may not
be with full or free will, it can never be without willing; and since the
willing is carried into effect, we cannot say that the actor was powerless.
If in yielding to compulsion you willed an act which you could not perform, we should say that the will was present, albeit forced, but the
power lacking. But when you do not act because you will not, the power
is there but the will is lacking, so long as your resistance to compulsion
withholds the act. That is why, in the employment either of compulsion
or of persuasion, it may be said: "Why not do what you have in your
power, in order to escape this evil?" And one who is altogether unable
to do that which he is being pressed to do on the supposition of his
ability, may reply with the excuse: "I would do it if it were in my power."
We have then a sufficient definition of power in the union of will with
the capacity to act. We say that any man has in his power that which he
does if he wills and does not if he wills not.

Now consider the question we raised for investigation: whether faith
is in our power. We are speaking of the faith with which we respond in
believing, not of that which we give when we make a promise. Here too
we speak of "faith," but we use the word in different senses when we say
"He had not faith in me," and when we say "He did not keep faith
with me": the meaning in the first case is: "He did not believe what I
said"; in the second, "He did not do what he said." By the faith wherewith we believe, we are faithful to God; by the faith wherewith his prom-
ises are performed, God himself is faithful to us: as the apostle says,
"God is faithful, in not suffering you to be tempted beyond that which
you are able." It is the faith whereby we believe God or believe in God,
of which we now ask whether it is in our power—the faith of which it is
written: "Abraham believed God, and it was counted unto him for

righteousness"; and again: "unto him that believeth in him that justifieth the ungodly, his faith is counted for righteousness."

Ask yourself, then, whether anyone can believe if he will not, or not believe if he will. The supposition is absurd—for belief is simply consenting to the truth of what is said, and consent is necessarily an act of will. It follows that faith must be in our power. But, as the apostle says, "there is no power but of God." There can be no reason, then, for excluding this power from the application of the words: "What hast thou which thou has not received?" Even our believing is a thing that God has granted to us. But nowhere do we read in the Holy Scriptures that "there is no will but of God"; and rightly so, for it is not true. Else, if there were no will but of him, God would be the author of sins—which God forbid! For the evil will by itself is sin, even if its effect be lacking, that is, if it have not power to act. When the evil will receives power to accomplish its intent, this comes of the judgment of God, in whom there is no unrighteousness: his punishment is carried out in this way as well as in others, and it is not the less just because it is hidden; though the wicked man only knows he is being punished, when manifest penalty makes him feel against his will the evil of the sin he wrought willingly. This is the meaning of what the apostle says of certain sinners: "God gave them over unto the lusts of their heart, to do the things which are unfitting." And as the Lord said to Pilate: "Thou couldest have no power against me, unless it were given thee from above." But the giving of power is not the imposition of necessity: the David who received the power to slay Saul, chose to spare and not to strike. Thus we understand that the evil receive power for the condemnation of their evil will, but the good for the proving of their good will.

Faith, then, is in our power, because everyone believes when he wills, and when he believes, believes willingly. We must next inquire, or rather recall to mind, what is the faith that the apostle urges upon us with such force of argument. It is not any kind of believing that is good; or we should not be warned: "Brethren, believe not every spirit; but test the spirit which is of God." Paul's words in his praise of charity, "believeth all things," do not mean that we should depreciate the charity of any man who does not at once believe everything he hears. The same charity forbids us easily to believe any evil of a brother, and counts it rather as a part of itself not to believe, when it hears such evil spoken. The charity that "believeth all things" also "believes not every spirit." We are not told that it believes all men: it believes all things, but its belief is given to God. There can be no doubt that the faith commended by the apostle is that whereby God is believed.

But a further distinction is required. God may be believed as well by those who are under the law and try to work their own righteousness through fear of punishment; so that they cannot work the righteousness of God. For that is done by the charity that takes pleasure only in the lawful, and not by the fear that is compelled to act lawfully, while the will's desire would be to have licence (if that were possible) for the unlawful. They also believe God: if they were devoid of such belief, they would have no dread of the law's punishment. But this is not the faith commended by the apostle, who says: "Ye have not received the spirit of bondage again unto fear, but ye have received the spirit of the adoption of sons, whereby we cry, Abba, Father." This fear then is the fear of slaves, and therefore, although it renders belief to the Master, there is in it no love of righteousness but only the fear of damnation. . . . This, finally, is the faith that works through love and not through fear, not dreading punishment but longing for righteousness. Whence comes that love, which is charity, through which faith works, but from the Source that granted it to faith's own petition? There could be no spark of it in us, however small, were it not shed abroad in our hearts through the Holy Spirit which is given to us. For this charity or love of God which is said to be shed abroad in our hearts is not his own love for us but that by which he makes us his lovers: like the righteousness of God by which we are made righteous through his gift, or the salvation of the Lord by which he causes us to be saved, or the faith of Jesus Christ by which he makes us faithful. That is the righteousness of God, which he does not only teach by the commandment of the law, but gives by the bestowal of the Spirit.

There is, however, a further question to which we should give some consideration. Is the will by which we believe also the gift of God, or is it exerted by the freedom of choice which is implanted in us by nature? If we say it is not God's gift, there is a danger of our supposing that we have found an answer to the apostle's rebuke: "What hast thou that thou hast not received? But if thou hast received it, why dost thou glory as though thou hadst not received it?" We may retort that we have the will to believe, which we have not received, and that gives us room to glory because we have not received it. If on the other hand we say that this act of will is nothing but the gift of God, again there will be danger lest the infidel and the godless be thought to have good ground for excusing their own unbelief on the plea that God has refused to grant them the will. When it is said that "it is God who worketh in us both to will and to work according to his good pleasure," we are already in the sphere of grace, granted to faith, in order that man may have the good works, worked by faith through the love which is shed abroad in our hearts by the Holy Spirit which is given to us. But in order that this grace may be granted we believe, and our belief is an act of will. It is of this will that we ask whence it comes. If by nature, then why not to all, since the same God is the Creator of all? If by the gift of God, still why not to all, since he will have all men to be saved and come to the knowledge of the truth?

Here the first point to be made, as a possible solution of the difficulty, is that the freedom of choice which the Creator has conferred in the way of nature upon the rational soul is a neutral power, which can either be exerted to faith or sink into unbelief. Accordingly it cannot be said that in the act of will whereby a man believes God, he possesses what he has not received, since it arises at God's call from the freedom of choice which he received in the way of nature at his creation. God wills all men to be saved and to come to the knowledge of the truth; but not so as to deprive them of that freedom of choice, for the good or evil use of which they are subject to the judgment of absolute Justice. By that judgment, the unbelieving act against God's will when they disbelieve his gospel; yet what they do is not to defeat his will but to cheat themselves of a supreme good and fall into the distress of punishment: in which they must learn the power of him whose mercy in his gifts they have despised. Thus the will of God is ever undefeated: which would not be, had he no way of dealing with his despisers, or were there any escape for them from his sentence upon such. Suppose a master say: "I will that all these my servants work in the vineyard, and after their labor rest and feast; provided that any who will not so work shall grind forever in the mill." It might appear that one who should despise the order is acting against his master's will; but he will only defeat it if in his master's despite he escapes also from the mill. And that under the power of God is altogether impossible. So it is written: "God spoke once"—which we understand in the sense of "unchangeably," though it might also be taken to mean a single utterance —and then we hear the matter of this unchangeable word: "these two things have I heard, that power belongeth unto God, and that mercy is thine, O Lord, who wilt render to every man according to his works." The despiser of his mercy, which calls for belief, must bear under his power the sentence of condemnation. But whosoever believes, and trusts himself to God for the absolution of all his sins, for the healing of all his sicknesses, for kindling and illumination by the warmth and light of God, shall have by his grace those good works which lead to deliverance even in the body from the corruption of death, to crowning and satisfaction with the good things which are not temporal but eternal, above all that we ask or think.

From *Summa Theologica*

ST. THOMAS AQUINAS

THE WILL

WHETHER THE WILL DESIRES SOMETHING OF NECESSITY

We proceed thus to the First Article:—
Objection 1. It would seem that the will desires nothing of necessity. For Augustine says that if anything is necessary, it is not voluntary. But whatever the will desires is voluntary. Therefore nothing that the will desires is desired of necessity.

Obj. 2. Further, *the rational powers,* according to the Philosopher, *extend to opposite things.* But the will is a rational power, because, as he says, *the will is in the reason.* Therefore the will extends to opposite things, and hence is determined to nothing of necessity.

Obj. 3. Further, by the will we are masters of our own actions. But we are not masters of that which is of necessity. Therefore the act of the will cannot be necessitated.

On the contrary, Augustine says that *all desire happiness with one will.* Now if this were not necessary, but contingent, there would at least be a few exceptions. Therefore the will desires something of necessity.

I answer that, The word *necessity* is employed in many ways. For that which must be is necessary. Now that a thing must be may belong to it by an intrinsic principle:—either material, as when we say that everything composed of contraries is of necessity corruptible;—or formal, as when we say that it is necessary for the three angles of a triangle to be equal to two right angles. And this is *natural* and *absolute necessity.* In another way, that a thing must be belongs to it by reason of something extrinsic, which is either the end or the agent. The necessity is imposed on something by the end when without it the end is not to be attained or so well attained: for instance, food is said to be necessary for life, and a horse is necessary for a journey. This is called the *necessity of the end,* and some-

From *Summa Theologica,* Part I, Question 82, articles 1, 2; Question 83, article 1. Part II, first part, Question 6, article 1. Printed in *Basic Writings of Saint Thomas Aquinas,* edited and annotated, with an introduction by A. C. Pegis (New York: Random House, Inc., 1945). Copyright 1945 by Random House, Inc. Reprinted by permission.

times also *utility*. The necessity is imposed by the agent when someone is forced by some agent, so that he is not able to do the contrary. This is called the *necessity of coercion*.

Now this necessity of coercion is altogether repugnant to the will. For we call *violent* that which is against the inclination of a thing. But the very movement of the will is an inclination to something. Therefore, just as a thing is called *natural* because it is according to the inclination of nature, so a thing is called *voluntary* because it is according to the inclination of the will. Therefore, just as it is impossible for a thing to be at the same time violent and natural, so it is impossible for a thing to be absolutely coerced, or violent, and voluntary.

But the necessity of the end is not repugnant to the will, when the end cannot be attained except in one way; and thus from the will to cross the sea arises in the will the necessity to desire a ship.

In like manner, neither is natural necessity repugnant to the will. Indeed, just as the intellect of necessity adheres to first principles, so the will must of necessity adhere to the last end, which is happiness; for the end is in practical matters what the principle is in speculative matters, as is said in *Physics*. For what befits a thing naturally and immovably must be the root and principle of all else pertaining thereto, since the nature of a thing is the first in everything, and every movement arises from something immovable.

Reply Obj. 1. The words of Augustine are to be understood of the necessity of coercion. But natural necessity *does not take away the liberty of the will,* as he himself says in the same work.

Reply Obj. 2. The will, so far as it desires a thing naturally, corresponds rather to the intellect of natural principles than to the reason, which extends to contraries. Hence, in this respect, it is rather an intellectual than a rational power.

Reply Obj. 3. We are masters of our own actions by reason of our being able to choose this or that. But choice regards, not the end, but *the means to the end,* as the Philosopher says. Consequently, the desire of the ultimate end is not among those actions of which we are masters.

WHETHER THE WILL DESIRES OF NECESSITY WHATEVER IT DESIRES

We proceed thus to the Second Article:—

Objection 1. It would seem that the will desires of necessity all that it desires. For Dionysius says that *evil is outside the scope of the will.* Therefore the will tends of necessity to the good which is proposed to it.

Obj. 2. Further, the object of the will is compared to the will as the mover to the movable thing. But the movement of the movable necessarily follows the mover. Therefore it seems that the will's object moves it of necessity.

Obj. 3. Further, just as the thing apprehended by sense is the object of the sensitive appetite, so the thing apprehended by the intellect is the object of the intellectual appetite, which is called the will. But what is apprehended by the sense moves the sensitive appetite of necessity, for Augustine says that *animals are moved by things seen.* Therefore it seems that whatever is apprehended by the intellect moves the will of necessity.

On the contrary, Augustine says that *it is the will by which we sin and live well.* Thus, the will extends to opposites. Therefore it does not desire of necessity all things whatsoever it desires.

I answer that, The will does not desire of necessity whatsoever it desires. In order to make this evident we must observe that, just as the intellect naturally and of necessity adheres to first principles, so the will adheres to the last end, as we have said already. Now there are some intelligible things which have no necessary connection with first principles: *e.g.,* contingent propositions, the denial of which does not involve a denial of first principles. And to such the intellect does not assent of necessity. But there are some propositions which have a necessary connection with first principles, namely, demonstrable conclusions, a denial of which involves a denial of first principles. And to these the intellect assents of necessity, when once it is aware (by demonstration) of the necessary connection of these conclusions with the principles; but it does not assent of necessity until through the demonstration it recognizes the necessity of such a connection.

It is the same with the will. For there are certain particular goods which have not a necessary connection with happiness, because without them a man can be happy; and to such the will does not adhere of necessity. But there are some things which have a necessary connection with happiness, namely, those by means of which man adheres to God, in Whom alone true happiness consists. Nevertheless, until through the certitude produced by seeing God the necessity of such a connection be shown, the will does not adhere to God of necessity, nor to those things which are of God. But the will of the man who sees God in His essence of necessity adheres to God, just as now we desire of necessity to be happy. It is therefore clear that the will does not desire of necessity whatever it desires.

Reply Obj. 1. The will can tend to nothing except under the aspect of good. But because good is of many kinds, for this reason the will is not of necessity determined to one.

Reply Obj. 2. The mover of necessity causes movement in the movable thing only when the power of the mover exceeds the movable thing in such a way that its entire capacity is subject to the mover. But as the capacity of the will is for the universal and perfect good, it is not subjected to any particular good. And therefore it is not of necessity moved by it.

Reply Obj. 3. The sensitive power does not compare different things with each other, as reason does; but it apprehends simply some one thing. Therefore, according to that one thing, it moves the sensitive appetite in a determinate way. But the reason is a power that compares several things together. Therefore the intellectual appetite—that is, the will— may be moved by several things, but not of necessity by one thing.

FREE CHOICE

WHETHER MAN HAS FREE CHOICE

We proceed thus to the First Article:—
Objection 1. It would seem that man has not free choice. For whoever has free choice does what he wills. But man does not what he wills, for it is written (*Rom.* vii. 19): *For the good which I will I do not, but the evil which I will not, that I do.* Therefore man has not free choice.

Obj. 2. Further, whoever has free choice has in his power to will or not to will, to do or not to do. But this is not in man's power, for it is written (*Rom.* ix. 16): *It is not of him that willeth*—namely, to will—*nor of him that runneth*—namely, to run. Therefore man has not free choice.

Obj. 3. Further, he is free who is his own master, as the Philosopher says. Therefore what is moved by another is not free. But God moves the will, for it is written (*Prov.* xxi. 1): *The heart of the king is in the hand of the Lord; whithersoever He will He shall turn it;* and (*Phil.* ii 13): *It is God Who worketh in you both to will and to accomplish.* Therefore man has not free choice.

Obj. 4. Further, whoever has free choice is master of his own actions. But man is not master of his own actions, for it is written (*Jer.* x. 23): *The way of a man is not his, neither is it in a man to walk.* Therefore man has not free choice.

Obj. 5. Further, the Philosopher says: *According as each one is, such does the end seem to him.* But it is not in our power to be such as we are, for this comes to us from nature. Therefore it is natural to us to follow some particular end, and therefore we are not free in so doing.

On the contrary, It is written (*Ecclus.* xv. 14): *God made man from the beginning, and left him in the hand of his own counsel;* and the *Gloss* adds: *That is, in the liberty of choice.*

I answer that, Man has free choice, or otherwise counsels, exhortations, commands, prohibitions, rewards and punishments would be in vain. In order to make this evident, we must observe that some things act without judgment, as a stone moves downwards; and in like manner all things which lack knowledge. And some act from judgment, but not a free judgment; as brute animals. For the sheep, seeing the wolf, judges it a thing to be shunned, from a natural and not a free judgment; because it judges, not from deliberation, but from natural instinct. And the same thing is to be said of any judgment in brute animals. But man acts from judgment, because by his apprehensive power he judges that something should be avoided or sought. But because this judgment, in the case of some particular act, is not from a natural instinct, but from some act of comparison in the reason, therefore he acts from free judgment and retains the power of being inclined to various things. For reason in contingent matters may follow opposite courses, as we see in dialectical syllogisms and rhetorical arguments. Now particular operations are contingent, and therefore in such matters the judgment of reason may follow opposite courses, and is not determinate to one. And in that man is rational, it is necessary that he have free choice.

Reply Obj. 1. As we have said above, the sensitive appetite, though it obeys the reason, yet in a given case can resist by desiring what the reason forbids. This is therefore the good which man does not when he wishes—namely, *not to desire against reason,* as Augustine says.

Reply Obj. 2. Those words of the Apostle are not to be taken as though man does not wish or does not run of his free choice, but because free choice is not sufficient thereto unless it be moved and helped by God.

Reply Obj. 3. Free choice is the cause of its own movement, because by his free choice man moves himself to act. But it does not of necessity belong to liberty that what is free should be the first cause of itself, as neither for one thing to be cause of another need it be the first cause. God, therefore, is the first cause, Who moves causes both natural and voluntary. And just as by moving natural causes He does not prevent their actions from being natural, so by moving voluntary causes He does not deprive their actions of being voluntary; but rather is He the cause of this very thing in them, for He operates in each thing according to its own nature.

Reply Obj. 4. *Man's way* is said *not to be his* in the execution of his choice, wherein he may be impeded, whether he will or not. The choice itself, however, is in us, but presupposes the help of God.

Reply Obj. 5. Quality in man is of two kinds: natural and adventitious. Now the natural quality may be in the intellectual part, or in the body and its powers. From the very fact, therefore, that man is such by virtue of a natural quality which is in the intellectual part, he naturally desires his last end, which is happiness. This desire is, indeed, a natural desire, and is not subject to free choice, as is clear from what we have said above. But on the part of the body and its powers, man may be such by virtue of a natural quality, inasmuch as he is of such a temperament or disposition due to any impression whatever produced by corporeal causes, which cannot affect the intellectual part, since it is not the act of a corporeal organ. And such as a man is by virtue of a corporeal quality, such also does his end seem to him, because from such a disposition a man is inclined to choose or reject something. But these inclinations are subject to the judgment of reason, which the lower appetite obeys, as we have said. Therefore this is in no way prejudicial to free choice.

The adventitious qualities are habits and passions, by virtue of which a man is inclined to one thing rather than to another. And yet even these inclinations are subject to the judgment of reasons. Such qualities, too, are subject to reason, as it is in our power either to acquire them, whether by causing them or disposing ourselves to them, or to reject them. And so there is nothing in this that is repugnant to free choice.

WHETHER THERE IS ANYTHING VOLUNTARY IN HUMAN ACTS

We proceed thus to the First Article:—
Objection 1. It would seem that there is nothing voluntary in human acts. For that is voluntary *which has its principle within itself,* as Gregory of Nyssa, Damascene and Aristotle declare. But the principle of human acts is not in man himself, but outside him, since man's appetite is moved to act by the appetible object which is outside him, and which is as a *mover unmoved.* Therefore there is nothing voluntary in human acts.

Obj. 2. Further, the Philosopher proves that in animals no new movement arises that is not preceded by another and exterior motion. But all human acts are new, since none is eternal. Consequently, the principle of all human acts is from outside man, and therefore there is nothing voluntary in them.

Obj. 3. Further, he that acts voluntarily can act of himself. But this is not true of man, for it is written (*Jo.* xv. 5): *Without Me you can do nothing.* Therefore there is nothing voluntary in human acts.

On the contrary, Damascene says that *the voluntary is an act consisting in a rational operation.* Now such are human acts. Therefore there is something voluntary in human acts.

I answer that, There must needs be something voluntary in human acts. In order to make this clear, we must take note that the principle of some acts is within the agent, or in that which is moved; whereas the principle of some movements or acts is outside. For when a stone is moved upwards, the principle of this movement is outside the stone; whereas, when it is moved downwards, the principle of this movement is in the stone. Now of those things that are moved by an intrinsic principle, some move themselves, some not. For since every agent or thing moved acts or is moved for an end, as was stated above, those are perfectly moved by an intrinsic principle whose intrinsic principle is one not only of movement but of movement for an end. Now in order that a thing be done for an end, some knowledge of the end is necessary. Therefore, whatever so acts or is so moved by an intrinsic principle that it has some knowledge of the end, has within itself the principle of its act, so that it not only acts, but acts for an end. On the other hand, if a thing has no knowledge of the end, even though it have an intrinsic principle of action or movement, nevertheless, the principle of acting or being moved for an end is not in that thing, but in something else, by which the principle of its action towards an end is imprinted on it. Therefore such things are not said to move themselves, but to be moved by others. But those things which have a knowledge of the end are said to move themselves because there is in them a principle by which they not only act but also act for an end. And, consequently, since both are from an intrinsic principle, *i.e.*, that they act and that they act for an end, the movements and acts of such things are said to be voluntary; for the term *voluntary* signifies that their movements and acts are from their own inclination. Hence it is that, according to the definitions of Aristotle, Gregory of Nyssa and Damascene, the voluntary is defined not only as having *a principle within* the agent, but also as implying *knowledge.* Therefore, since man especially knows the end of his work, and moves himself, in his acts especially is the voluntary to be found.

Reply Obj. 1. Not every principle is a first principle. Therefore, although it is of the nature of the voluntary act that its principle be within the agent, nevertheless, it is not contrary to the nature of the voluntary act that this intrinsic principle be caused or moved by an extrinsic principle; for it is not of the nature of the voluntary act that its intrinsic principle be a first principle.—Nevertheless, it must be observed that a principle of movement may happen to be first in a genus, but not first absolutely. Thus, in the genus of things subject to alteration, the first principle of alteration is the body of the heavens, which nevertheless is not the first mover absolutely, but is moved locally by a higher mover. And so the intrinsic principle of the voluntary act, *i.e.*, the cognitive and appetitive power, is the first principle in the genus of appetitive movement, although it is moved by an extrinsic principle according to other species of movement.

Reply Obj. 2. New movements in animals are indeed preceded by a motion from without; and this in two respects. First, in so far as by means of an extrinsic motion an animal's senses are confronted with something sensible, which, on being apprehended, moves the appetite. Thus a lion, on seeing the approach of the stag through its movement, begins to be moved towards the stag.—Secondly, in so far as some extrinsic motion produces a physical change in an animal's body, for example, through cold or heat; and when the body is thus affected by the motion of an exterior body, the sensitive appetite likewise, which is the power of a bodily organ, is moved accidentally. Thus, it happens that through some alteration in the body the appetite is roused to the desire of something. But this is not contrary to the nature of voluntariness, as was stated above, for such movements caused by an extrinsic principle are of another genus of movement.

Reply Obj. 3. God moves man to act, not only by proposing the appetible to the senses, or by effecting a change in his body, but also by moving the will itself; for every movement both of the will and of nature proceeds from God as the First Mover. And just as it is not incompatible with nature that the movement of nature be from God as the First Mover, inasmuch as nature is an instrument of God moving it, so it is not contrary to the character of a voluntary act that it proceed from God, inasmuch as the will is moved by God. Nevertheless, both natural and voluntary movements have this in common, that it belongs to the nature of both that they should proceed from a principle within the agent.

From *The Oxford Commentary*

JOHN DUNS SCOTUS

The Question is proposed.—With regard to the twenty-fifth distinction I ask one thing: *Whether anything other than the will effectively causes the act of willing in the will?*

Principal Arguments. I argue for the affirmative: (a) In Book III of the *De Anima* Aristotle lays down an order of what moves and what is moved, thus: the desirable object is an unmoved mover; the appetite is a moved mover, moved, that is, by the desirable object; and in the third place is that which is moved but is not a mover, namely, that which is moved by the act and the command of the will or of the appetite, as is the body of an animal.—It cannot be said that the desirable object moves *metaphorically,* as an *end* moves; because then the Philosopher would at once *equivocate* about the activation of movement, when he says that the first, for instance the desirable object, moves the second, namely the appetite, and the second, namely the appetite, moves the third, because the second, namely the appetite, moves *properly.* And in what is ordered essentially, it seems that the middle should be moved by the first by that kind of movement by which the last is moved by the middle. . . .

(d) Also, what is of itself undetermined to one of opposing alternatives; . . . does not act unless a determining agent concurs, because as undetermined it is not more disposed to be effected than not to be. But the will of itself is disposed in this way to its act; so another agent must be given, which does not seem to be unless it is the object.

To the Contrary: In Augustine's twelfth book of the *City of God,* chapter 6, he says that if two men are equally affected in soul and body, and they are then tempted by the same beauty or object, whence is it that one falls and the other does not? And he says that this is only from the *will.* . . .

(c) Also, Augustine says in Book II of *On Free Choice* that unless those actions which are voluntary for us were placed in our power, the will should be neither praised nor blamed, nor admonished. And he who says or feels that the will is not to be admonished should be cut off from the number of men.

From *The Oxford Commentary on the Four Books of the Master of the Sentences,* Book II, Distinction XXV, The Single Question, translated by James Walsh.

(d) I argue therefore thus: Insofar as a patient is passive, it is not in its power to be affected. Proof: A patient is only affected because an agent acts; but the prior is not in the power of the posterior; therefore the action of the agent is not in the power of the patient; therefore, neither is its passion. Proof: If the agent acts, the patient is necessarily affected. Therefore, if the will is only *receptive* and passive with respect to its volition, no volition is in its *power*. Therefore, etc. . . .

The Position is Expounded Which Holds That the Active Cause of Volition is the Object as Known. There is *another opinion* of an *older* Doctor which reaches the same conclusion, namely, that the will *is moved by something else;* but it holds that this something else is the *object known* or understood. . . .

(b) Also, the *sensitive* appetite is moved effectively by the *sensible* desirable thing; therefore the *intellective* is moved by the *intelligible* desirable things.

(c) *If you say* against this that *what does not exist* cannot be the cause of any *being;* but the intelligible object can be a *non-being* absolutely in itself; and so it cannot be the cause of the will, *they reply* that the object *as known* does act as a cause, and this is to say that the *intellect* through its act of understanding causes volition, and so it cannot be that such a cause should be *nothing.* For abstractive cognition is not *nothing* in the intellect, even though the object might not exist in itself or in an outside thing.

The Common Conclusion of Both Positions is Opposed. These two opinions agree in that they hold that something *other than the will moves it*; but as is obvious, they disagree as to the mover.

Against the *conclusion* itself there are principal arguments, and I reply by arguing from them thus:

(a) A *natural* agent cannot by itself be the cause of contraries with respect to the *same* patient (which excludes the case of something *melting ice* and *drying mud at the same time*); but it is in the power of our will to have *negative* and *positive volition,* which are contraries, with respect to a *single object.* Therefore these cannot be produced by an agent *naturally;* and therefore not by the *object,* which is a *natural* agent. Assume, therefore, that the *object* is the cause of the *positive volition.* Still, something else would have to be the cause of the *negative volition.* But that something other than the will could only be the *evil* object. But evil, since it is a *privation,* could not be the cause of a *positive* act, and *negative volition* is such a positive act. Therefore it must be effectively from the will. . . .

(c) *It is said* that volition is in the power of the will insofar as it can *determine the intellect* to the consideration or avoidance of this or that; and volition is thus in the power of the will, except insofar as the *first* act is concerned.

To the Contrary: I agree that the first action in the will is caused by the object, whatever that might be which has to be held according to you. That action is purely *natural;* and therefore it is not in the *power* of the will. For it is not in our power that we should not be touched by what we see, according to Augustine. Therefore if after that act *I am able to move the intellect* to the consideration of this or that, I ask, by *what act?* Not by this one, because this one is not in the *power* of the will. Then it must be by another. Concerning that other I ask, *from whence* is it? It is either from the *will* itself, or from the *object,* or from the *phantasm.* If from the *will,* I have my position, because then that *volition* is in its *power* and *is effectively* from the will, and by the same argument so is the *first volition.* Or else it is from *something else,* namely from the object or the phantasm; and if so, then it will be a *natural* act, and as a consequence it will no longer be in the power of the will so to command the intellect concerning the consideration of this or that any more than was the *first* act. . . .

(e) *Others say* to the *argument* that the object of the intellect occurs under a two-fold aspect, namely under the aspect of the *illicit* and under the aspect of the *delectable,* as is obvious in the object of fornication. And then it is in the *power* of the will to arrest the intellect in what is shameful, dismissing the other, and then follows the evil choice.

To the Contrary: I ask, do these two aspects move *equally,* or not? If *equally,* then they will cause *negative* and *positive volition* in the will *at the same time* with respect to *the same object,* which is impossible. If they move *unequally,* then one of them moves the will *more efficaciously,* and it does this *naturally* and *necessarily,* and, as a consequence that volition will not be in the *power* of the will, but according to that it will also move the intellect necessarily. Therefore it will not be able to arrest it in the other aspect. . . .

The Second Argument of the First Position is Resolved. (a) To the *other* argument from the non-coincidence of the material and efficient causes, *it is said* that we can consider a duality in the will: insofar as it is *appetite* or insofar as it is *free.* Insofar as it is free it is *productive,* insofar as it is appetite it is *receptive;* so that there is here a *difference of intention* regarding the will. . . .

(b) *I do not take this well;* because the proximate reason for constituting a species, such as is the ultimate differentia, is the proximate reason for having a proper passion. For man does not have his *ability to laugh* by reason of being an *animal,* but by reason of being *rational.* But *freedom* rather than *appetite* is the more formal defining feature of the will; and so just as *freedom* is more of a *constitutive feature* of the will, so it defines the *kind of receptivity* appropriate to the will. . . .

The Arguments of the Second Position are Resolved. . . . (b) To the *other* one concerning the *sensitive appetite* which is moved by the desirable object, *I say* that it is just the opposite. For the sensitive appetite is moved in this way because it is not *free,* but the other is free. Whence

Damascene says in chapter 42 that the sensitive *is led* and does not lead, but the intellective *leads*, and is not led.

It is Shown that Nothing Other than the Will is the Total Cause of Volition. *I say* then to the *question* that *nothing other than the will is the total cause of volition in the will.* One argument, outside of the ones previously mentioned, is this: something happens in things *contingently.* And I call an *avoidable* event a *contingent* event. Otherwise, if everything happened *inevitably,* it would not be appropriate to give advice, nor to negotiate, as Aristotle says in I of the *De Interpretatione.* I ask, then, whence or from *what cause* that which happens *contingently* happens? Not by a *determined* cause, because for that instant for which it is so *determined* the effect cannot happen *contingently;* therefore it happens by a cause *undetermined* to *one or the other* of opposing alternatives. Then, either that cause can determine *itself contingently* to *one* of the alternatives, since it cannot do so to *both at once,* as Aristotle says in IX of the *Metaphysics* concerning *rational potency,* or it cannot determine itself, but *something else* determines it to one of those. If *it can* determine itself to one of those contingently or not inevitably, the position is had. If it is determined to one of those *by something else,* then it is determined either *necessarily,* or *contingently.* If *necessarily,* the effect happens *inevitably.* If the determining factor determines to one of those *contingently* and avoidably, so that it could determine to the other, such a determining factor can only be the *will,* because every *natural* active cause is *determined* to *one* effect, or if a natural cause is *undetermined,* it can neither determine itself nor another.

It is Shown that the Indetermination of the Will is Not on the Part of the Intellect. You say: this *indetermination* is on the part of the *intellect,* in so representing the object to the will, as it *will be* or *will not be.*

To the Contrary: (a) The intellect cannot determine the will indifferently to either of contradictories (for instance, this *will be* or *will not be*), except by demonstrating one and constructing a paralogism or a sophistical syllogism regarding the other, so that in drawing the conclusion it is deceived. Therefore if that contingency by which this can be or not be were from the intellect, dictating in this way by means of opposite conclusions, then nothing would happen contingently by the will of God or by God, because He does not construct paralogisms nor is He deceived. But this is false. . . .

(b) Also, the intellect acts in a way which is most of all *natural;* see Augustine, III of *On the Trinity* and in many other places. Here he posits the intellect as the appropriated principle with respect to the production of the Son in the Divine Persons, Who is produced most *naturally* of all. The intellect, then, is least of all an *undetermined* cause of any effect; rather, it is a *determined* cause.

(c) *You say:* The Philosopher distinguishes *nature* as against *intellect* and as against acting *by intention.* Therefore he does not understand that the *intellect* is a cause in the manner of *nature*. *I say* that *intellect* can be taken either *in itself*, according to which it is a certain *operative power* of such an operation, distinguished as against the operation of the *will*, and therefore inasmuch as it is from itself it acts *naturally;* or it can be taken in the way according to which it is a *practical* power with respect to what can be done externally. And so for the *same thing* the Philosopher has *art, understanding, purpose, choice*, and *appetite*. And it is in taking *intellect* in this way that he distinguishes acting by *intellect* as against acting by *nature*. . . .

The Principal Arguments are Resolved. (a) To the *first principal argument*, which would say that the *object* moves the will *effectively*, not as a *total* cause, but as producing something there; were the authority not then glossed "which moves, namely *metaphorically*," then the authority would be for me. Or else in sustaining and saying that the desirable object moves the appetite at least *metaphorically*, then it ought to be understood that just as the desirable object moves the appetite metaphorically, so the appetite thus moved moves the limbs *effectively* to pursue and obtain that object. And *when it is said* that *he equivocates* concerning what moves, *this avails nothing;* because it is not required that everything ordered according to the criterion of *causation* should be ordered in *one type of cause*. For the *efficient* cause is ordered to the *final*, which is a cause of the *other* type, which moves *metaphorically*. From which it can be said that Aristotle assigns there an order of causes of any kind of movement whatsoever. . . .

(d) To the *other* argument concerning the *potency of contradiction*, which argument is that it is not in the potency of contradiction to anything that it should *determine itself* to one of those alternatives, I say that there is a certain form of the potency of contradiction, such as *science*, which is of contraries, and this form is not able to determine itself because it is *diminished* and *imperfect* insofar as it has regard to both contraries. Whence Aristotle wished to say that if it should proceed to act from itself, without anything else determining it, it would produce contraries at the same time. There is a different form of potency which is still undetermined after the object has been presented to it, which is *perfect*, however, and *not diminished*. The *will* is of this kind, and this kind can *determine itself* and also *the other kind*. Whence in Book IX of the *Metaphysics*, after saying that science is of contraries and cannot determine itself to one of them, Aristotle added the determining factor: *but this I call appetite or choice*. Therefore the *perfect* rational power, such as the *will*, even though it is a potency of contradictories, can *determine itself* to one of them, once the object has been presented.

From *The Questions Concerning Liberty, Necessity, and Chance*

THOMAS HOBBES

T. H. Whether whatsoever comes to pass proceed from *necessity,* or some things from *chance,* has been a question disputed amongst the old philosophers long time before the incarnation of our Saviour, without drawing into argument on either side the almighty power of the Deity. But the third way of bringing things to pass, distinct from *necessity* and *chance,* namely, *freewill,* is a thing that never was mentioned amongst them, nor by the Christians in the beginning of Christianity. For St. Paul, that disputes that question largely and purposely, never useth the term *freewill;* nor did he hold any doctrine equivalent to that which is now called the doctrine of freewill; but deriveth all actions from the irresistible will of God, and nothing from the will of him that *runneth or willeth.* But for some ages past, the doctors of the Roman Church have exempted from this dominion of God's will the will of man; and brought in a doctrine, that not only man, but also his will is free, and determined to this or that action, not by the will of God, nor necessary causes, but by the power of the will itself. And though by the reformed Churches instructed by Luther, Calvin, and others, this opinion was cast out, yet not many years since it began again to be reduced by Arminius and his followers, and became the readiest way to ecclesiastical promotion; . . .

J. D. Either I am free to write this discourse for liberty against necessity, or I am not free. If I be free, I have obtained the cause, and ought not to suffer for the truth. If I be not free, yet I ought not to be blamed, since I do it not out of any voluntary election, but out of an inevitable necessity. . . .

From *The Questions concerning Liberty, Necessity, and Chance,* clearly stated and debated between Dr. Bramhall, Bishop of Derry and Thomas Hobbes of Malmesbury. Printed in The English Works of Thomas Hobbes, Vol. V, Sir William Molesworth, Bart., editor. (London: John Bohn, 1841.)

T. H. The preface is a handsome one, but it appears even in that, that he hath mistaken the question; for whereas he says thus, "if I be free to write this discourse, I have obtained the cause," I deny that to be true. For it is not enough to his freedom of writing that he had not written it, unless he would himself; if he will obtain the cause, he must prove that, before he wrote it, it was not necessary he should write it afterwards. It may be he thinks it all one to say, "I was free to write it," and "it was not necessary I should write it." But I think otherwise; for he is free to do a thing, that may do it if he have the will to do it, and may forbear if he have the will to forbear. And yet if there be a necessity that he shall have the will to do it, the action is necessarily to follow; and if there be a necessity that he shall have the will to forbear, the forbearing also will be necessary. The question, therefore, is not whether a man be a free agent, that is to say, whether he can write or forbear, speak or be silent, according to his will; but whether the will to write, and the will to forbear, come upon him according to his will, or according to any thing else in his own power. I acknowledge this liberty, that I can do if I will: but to say, I can will if I will, I take to be an absurd speech. Wherefore I cannot grant him the cause upon this preface.

J. D. . . . (a) Thus much I will maintain, that that is no true necessity, which he calls necessity; nor that liberty, which he calls liberty; nor that the question, which he makes the question.

First for liberty, that which he calls liberty, is no true liberty.

For the clearing whereof, it behoveth us to know the difference between these three, *necessity, spontaneity,* and *liberty.*

Necessity and spontaneity may sometimes meet together; so may spontaneity and liberty; but real necessity and true liberty can never meet together. Some things are necessary and not voluntary or spontaneous; some things are both necessary and voluntary; some things are voluntary and not free; some things are both voluntary and free; but those things which are truly necessary can never be free, and those things which are truly free can never be necessary. Necessity consists in an antecedent determination to one; spontaneity consists in a conformity of the appetite, either intellectual or sensitive, to the object; true liberty consists in the elective power of the rational will; that which is determined without my concurrence, may nevertheless agree well enough with my fancy or desires, and obtain my subsequent consent; but that which is determined without my concurrence or consent, cannot be the object of mine election. I may like that which is inevitably imposed upon me by another, but if it be inevitably imposed upon me by extrinsical causes, it is both folly for me to deliberate, and impossible for me to choose, whether I shall undergo it or not. Reason is the root, the fountain, the original of true liberty, which judgeth and representeth to the will, whether this or that be convenient, whether this or that be more convenient. Judge then what a pretty kind of liberty it is which is maintained by T. H., such a liberty as is in little children before they have the use of reason, before they can consult or deliberate of any thing. Is not this a childish liberty; and such a liberty as is in brute beasts, as bees and spiders, which do not learn their faculties as we do our trades, by experience and consideration? This is a brutish liberty, such a liberty as a bird hath to fly when her wings are clipped, or to use his own comparison, such a liberty as a lame man, who hath lost the use of his limbs, hath to walk. Is not this a ridiculous liberty? Lastly, (which is worse than all these), such a liberty as a river hath to descend down the channel. What! will he ascribe liberty to inanimate creatures also, which have neither reason, nor spontaneity, nor so much as sensitive appetite? Such is T. H.'s liberty.

(b) His necessity is just such another, a necessity upon supposition, arising from the concourse of all the causes, including the last dictate of the understanding in reasonable creatures. The adequate cause and the effect are together in time, and when all the concurrent causes are determined, the effect is determined also, and is become so necessary that it is actually in being; but there is a great difference between determining, and being determined. If all the collateral causes concurring to the production of an effect, were antecedently determined what they must of necessity produce, and when they must produce it, then there is no doubt but the effect is necessary. (c) But if these causes did operate freely or contingently; if they might have suspended or denied their concurrence, or have concurred after another manner, then the effect was not truly and antecedently necessary, but either free or contingent. This will be yet clearer by considering his own instance of *casting ambs ace,* though it partake more of contingency than of freedom. Supposing the positure of the parties' hand who did throw the dice, supposing the figure of the table and of the dice themselves, supposing the measure of force applied, and supposing all other things which did concur to the production of that cast, to be the very same they were, there is no doubt but in this case the cast is necessary. But still this is but a necessity of supposition; for if all these concurrent causes, or some of them, were contingent or free, then the cast was not absolutely necessary. To begin with the caster, he might have denied his concurrence, and not have cast at all; he might have suspended his concurrence, and not have cast so soon; he might have doubled or diminished his force in casting, if it had pleased him; he might have thrown the dice into the other table. In all these cases what becomes of his *ambs-ace?* The like uncertainties offer themselves for the maker of the tables, and for the maker of the dice, and for the keeper of the tables, and for the kind of wood, and I know not how many other circumstances. In such a mass of contingencies, it is impossible that the effect should be antecedently necessary. T. H. appeals to every man's experience. I am contented. Let every one reflect upon himself, and he shall find no convincing, much less constraining reason, to necessitate him to any one of these particular acts more than another, but only his own will or arbitrary determination. So T. H.'s necessity is no absolute, no antecedent, extrinsical necessity, but merely a necessity upon supposition.

(d) Thirdly, that which T. H. makes the question, is not the question. 'The question is not,' saith he, 'whether a man may write if he will, and forbear if he will, but whether the will to write or the will to forbear come upon him according to his will, or according to anything else in his own power.' Here is a distinction without a difference. If his will do not come upon him according to his will, then he is not a free, nor yet so much as a voluntary agent, which is T. H.'s liberty. Certainly all the freedom of the agent is from the freedom of the will. If the will have no power over itself, the agent is no more free than a staff in a man's hand. Secondly, he makes but an empty show of power in the will, either to write or not to write. (e) If it be precisely and inevitably determined in all occurrences whatsoever, what a man shall will, and what he shall not will, what he shall write, and what he shall not write, to what purpose is this power? God and nature never made any thing in vain; but vain and frustraneous is that power which never was and never shall be deduced into act. Either the agent is determined before he acteth, what he shall will, and what he shall not will, what he shall act, and what he shall not act, and then he is no more free to act than he is to will; or else he is not determined, and then there is no necessity. No effect can exceed the virtue of its cause; if the action be free to write or to forbear, the power or faculty to will or nill must of necessity be more free. *Quod efficit tale, illud magis est tale.* If the will be determined, the writing or not writing is likewise determined, and then he should not say, 'he may write or he may forbear,' but he must write or he must forbear. Thirdly, this answer contradicts the sense of all the world, that the will of man is determined without his will, or without any thing in his power. Why do we ask men whether they will do such a thing or not? Why do we represent reasons to them? Why do we pray them? Why do we entreat them? Why do we blame them, if their will come not upon them according to their will. *Wilt thou be made clean?* said our Saviour to the paralytic person (John v. 6); to what purpose, if his will was extrinsically determined? Christ complains, (Matth. xi. 17): *We have piped unto you, and ye have not danced.* How could they help it, if their wills were determined without their wills to forbear? And (Matth. xxiii. 37): *I would have gathered your children together as the hen gathereth her chickens under her wings, but ye would not.* How easily might they answer, according to T. H.'s doctrine, 'Alas! blame not us; our wills are not in our own power or disposition; if they were, we would thankfully embrace so great a favour.' Most truly said St. Austin, 'Our will should not be a will at all, if it were not in our power.' (f) This is the belief of all mankind, which we have not learned from our tutors, but is imprinted in our hearts by nature; we need not turn over any obscure books to find out this truth. The poets chaunt it in the theatres, the shepherds in the mountains, the pastors teach it in their churches, the doctors in the universities, the common people in the markets, and all mankind in the whole world do assent unto it, except an handful of men who have poisoned their intellectuals with paradoxical principles. Fourthly, this necessity which T. H. hath devised, which is grounded upon the necessitation of a man's will without his will, is the worst of all others, and is so far from lessening those difficulties and absurdities which flow from the fatal destiny of the Stoics, that it increaseth them, and rendereth them unanswerable. (g) No man blameth fire for burning whole cities; no man taxeth poison for destroying men; but those persons who apply them to such wicked ends. If the will of man be not in his own disposition, he is no more a free agent than the fire or the poison. Three things are required to make an act or omission culpable. First, that it be in our power to perform it or forbear it; secondly, that we be obliged to perform it, or forbear it, respectively; thirdly, that we omit that which we ought to have done, or do that which we ought to have omitted. (h) No man sins in doing those things which he could not shun, or forbearing those things which never were in his power. T. H. may say, that besides the power, men have also an appetite to evil objects, which render them culpable. It is true; but if this appetite be determined by another, not by themselves, or if they have not the use of reason to curb or restrain their appetites, they sin no more than a stone descending downward, according to its natural appetite, or the brute beasts who commit voluntary errors in following their sensitive appetites, yet sin not.

(i) The question then is not whether a man be necessitated to will or nill, yet free to act or forbear. But saving the ambiguous acception of the word *free,* the question is plainly this, whether all agents, and all events natural, civil, moral, (for we speak not now of the conversion of a sinner, that concerns not this question), be predetermined extrinsically and inevitably without their own concurrence in the determination; so as all actions and events which either are or shall be, cannot but be, nor can be otherwise, after any other manner, or in any other place, time, number, measure, order, nor to any other end, than they are. And all this in respect of the supreme cause, or a concourse of extrinsical causes determining them to one.

(k) So my preface remains yet unanswered. Either I was extrinsically and inevitably predetermined to write this discourse, without any concurrence of mine in the determination, and without any power in me to change or oppose it, or I was not so predetermined. If I was, then I ought not to be blamed, for no man is justly blamed for doing that which never was in his power to shun. If I was not so predetermined, then mine actions and my will to act, are neither compelled nor necessitated by any extrinsical causes, but I elect and choose, either to write or to forbear, according to mine own will and mine own power. And when I have resolved and elected, it is but a necessity of supposition, which may and doth consist with true liberty, not a real antecedent necessity. The two horns of this dilemma are so straight, that no mean can be given, nor room to pass between them. And the two consequences are so evident, that instead of answering he is forced to decline them.

T. H. (*a*) "Thus much I will maintain, that this is no true necessity, which he calleth necessity; nor that liberty which he calleth liberty; nor that the question, which he makes the question," &C. "For the clearing whereof, it behoveth us to know the difference between these three, *necessity, spontaneity,* and *liberty.*"

I did expect, that for the knowing of the difference between *necessity, spontaneity,* and *liberty,* he would have set down their definitions. For without these, their difference cannot possibly appear. For how can a man know how things differ, unless he first know what they are? which he offers not to shew. He tells us that *necessity* and *spontaneity* may meet together, and *spontaneity* and *liberty*; but *necessity* and *liberty* never; and many other things impertinent to the purpose. For which, because of the length, I refer the reader to the place. I note only this, that *spontaneity* is a word not used in common English; and they that understand Latin, know it means no more than *appetite,* or *will,* and is not found but in living creatures. And seeing, he saith, that *necessity* and *spontaneity* may stand together, I may say also, that *necessity* and *will* may stand together, and then is not the will free, as he would have it, from necessitation? There are many other things in that which followeth, which I had rather the reader would consider in his own words, to which I refer him, than that I should give him greater trouble in reciting them again. For I do not fear it will be thought too hot for my fingers, to shew the vanity of such words as these, *intellectual appetite, conformity of the appetite to the object, rational will, elective power of the rational will*; nor understand I how reason can be the root of true liberty, if the Bishop, as he saith in the beginning, had the liberty to write this discourse. I understand how objects, and the conveniences and the inconveniences of them may be represented to a man, by the help of his senses; but how reason representeth anything to the will, I understand no more than the Bishop understands how there may be liberty in children, in beasts, and inanimate creatures. For he seemeth to wonder how children may be left at liberty; how beasts in prison may be set at liberty; and how a river may have a free course; and saith, "What! will be ascribe liberty to inanimate creatures, also?" And thus he thinks he hath made it clear how *necessity, spontaneity,* and *liberty* differ from one another. If the reader find it so, I am contented.

(b) "His necessity is just such another; a necessity upon supposition, arising from the concourse of all the causes, including the last dictate of the understanding in reasonable creatures," &c.

The Bishop might easily have seen, that the necessity I hold, is the same necessity that he denies; namely, a necessity of things future, that is, an antecedent necessity derived from the very beginning of time; and that I put necessity for an impossibility of not being, and that impossibility as well as possibility are never truly said but of the future. I know as well as he that the cause, when it is adequate, as he calleth it, or entire, as I call it, is together in time with the effect. But for all that, the necessity may be and is before the effect, as much as any necessity can be. And though he call it a necessity of supposition, it is no more so than all other necessity is. The fire burneth necessarily; but not without supposition that there is fuel put to it. And it burneth the fuel, when it is put to it, necessarily; but it is by supposition, that the ordinary course of nature is not hindered; for the fire burnt not the three children in the furnace.

(c) "But if these causes did operate freely or contingently, if they might have suspended or denied their concurrence, or have concurred after another manner, then the effect was not truly and antecedently necessary, but either free or contingent."

It seems by this he understands not what these words, *free* and *contingent,* mean. A little before, he wondered I should attribute liberty to inanimate creatures, and now he puts causes amongst those things that operate freely. By these causes it seems he understandeth only men, whereas I shewed before that liberty is usually ascribed to whatsoever agent is not hindered. And when a man doth any thing freely, there be many other agents immediate, that concur to the effect he intendeth, which work not freely, but necessarily; as when the man moveth the sword *freely,* the sword woundeth necessarily, nor can suspend or deny its concurrence; and consequently if the man move not himself, the man cannot deny his concurrence. To which he cannot reply unless he say a man originally can move himself; for which he will be able to find no authority of any that have but tasted of the knowledge of motion. Then for *contingent,* he understandeth not what it meaneth. For it is all one to say it is *contingent,* and simply to say *it is;* saying that when they say simply *it is,* they consider not how or by what means; but in saying it is *contingent,* they tell us they know not whether necessarily or not. But the Bishop thinking contingent to be that which is not necessary, instead of arguing against our knowledge of the necessity of things to come, argueth against the necessity itself. Again, he supposeth that free and contingent causes might have suspended or denied their concurrence. From which it followeth, that free causes, and contingent causes, are not causes of themselves, but concurrent with other causes, and therefore can produce nothing but as they are guided by those causes with which they concur. For it is strange he should say, they might have concurred after another manner; for I conceive not how, when this runneth one way, and that another, that they can be said to concur, that is, run together. And this his concurrence of causes contingent, maketh, he saith, the cast of *ambs-ace* not to have been absolutely necessary. Which cannot be conceived, unless it had hindered it; and then it had made some other cast necessary, perhaps *deux-ace,* which serveth me well. For that which he saith of suspending his concurrence, of casting sooner or later, of altering the caster's force, and the like accidents, serve not to take away the necessity of *ambs-ace,* otherwise than by making a necessity of *deux-ace,* or other cast that shall be thrown.

(*d*) "Thirdly, that which T. H. makes the question, is not the question," &c.

He hath very little reason to say this. He requested me to tell him my opinion in writing concerning free-will. Chich I did, and did let him know aman was free, in those things that were in his power, to follow his will; but that he was not free to will, that is, that his will did not follow his will. Which I expressed in these words: "The question is, whether the will to write, or the will to forbear, come upon a man according to his will, or according to any thing else in his own power." He that cannot understand the difference between *free to do if he will,* and *free to will,* is not fit, as I have said in the stating of the question, to hear this controversy disputed, much less to be a writer in it. His consequence, "if a man be not free to will, he is not free nor a voluntary agent," and his saying, "the freedom of the agent is from the freedom of the will," is put here without proof; nor is there any considerable proof of it through the whole book hereafter offered. For why? He never before had heard, I believe, of any distinction between free to do and free to will; which makes him also say, "if the will have not power over itself, the agent is no more free, than a staj in a man's hand." As if it were not freedom enough for a man to do what he will, unless his will also have power over his will, and that his will be not the power itself, but must have another power within it to do all voluntary acts.

(*e*) "If it be precisely and inevitably determined in all occurrences whatsoever, what a man shall will, and what he shall not will, and what he shall write, and what he shall not write, to what purpose is this power?" &c.

It is to this purpose, that all those things may be brought to pass, which God hath from eternity predetermined. It is therefore to no purpose here to say, that God and nature hath made nothing in vain. But see what weak arguments he brings next, which, though answered in that which is gone before, yet, if I answer not again, he will say they are too hot for my fingers. One is: "If the agent be determined what he shall will, and what he shall act, then he is no more free to act than he is to will"; as if the will being necessitated, the doing of what we will were not liberty. Another is: "If a man be free to act, he is much more free to will because *quod efficit tale, illud magis est tale*"; as if he should say, "if I make him angry, then I am more angry; because *quod efficit*." &c. The third is: "If the will be determined, then the writing is determined, and he ought not to say he *may* write, but he *must* write." It is true, it followeth that he must write, but it doth not follow I ought to say he must write, unless he would have me say more than I know, as himself doth often in this reply.

After his arguments come his difficult question, "If the will of man be determined without his will or without any thing in his power, why do we ask men whether they will do such a thing or not?" I answer, because we desire to know, and cannot know but by their telling, nor then neither, for the most part. "Why do we represent reasons to them? Why do we pray them? Why do we entreat them?" I answer, because thereby we think to make them have the will they have not. "Why do we blame them?" I answer, because they please us not. I might ask him, whether blaming be any thing else but saying the thing blamed is ill or imperfect? May we not say a horse is lame, though his lameness came from necessity? or that a man is a fool or a knave, if he be so, though he could not help it? "To what purpose did our Saviour say to the paralytic person, *wilt thou be made clean,* if his will were extrinsically determined?" I answer, that it was not because he would know, for he knew it before; but because he would draw from him a confession of his want. "*We have piped unto you, and ye have not danced;* how could they help it?" I answer they could not help it. "*I would have gathered your children as the hen gathereth her chickens under her wings, but ye would not.* How easily might they answer, according to T. H.'s doctrine, Alas! blame not us, our wills are not in our own power?" I answer, they are to be blamed though their wills be not in their own power. Is not good good, and evil evil, though they be not in our power? and shall not I call them so? and is not that praise and blame? But it seems the Bishop takes blame, not for the dispraise of a thing, but for a pretext and colour of malice and revenge against him he blameth. And where he says our wills are in our power, he sees not that he speaks absurdly; for he ought to say, the will is the power; and through ignorance detecteth the same fault in St. Austin, who saith, "our will should not be a will at all, if it were not in our power;" that is to say, if it were not in our will.

(*f*) "This is the belief of all mankind, which we have not learned from our tutors, but is imprinted in our hearts by nature," &c.

This piece of eloquence is used by Cicero in his defence of Milo, to prove it lawful for a man to resist force with force, or to keep himself from killing; which the Bishop, thinking himself able to make that which proves one thing prove any thing, hath translated into English, and brought into this place to prove free-will. It is true, very few have learned from tutors, that a man is not free to will; nor do they find it much in books. That they find in books, that which the poets chant in their theatres and the shepherds in the mountains, that which the pastors teach in the churches and the doctors in the universities, and that which the common people in the markets, and all mankind in the whole world do assent unto, is the same that I assent unto, namely, that a man hath freedom to do if he will; but whether he hath freedom to will, is a question which it seems neither the Bishop nor they ever thought on.

(*g*) "No man blameth fire for burning cities nor taxeth poison for destroying men," &c.

Here again he is upon his arguments from blame which I have answered before; and we do as much blame them as we do men. For we say fire hath done hurt, and the poison hath killed a man as well as we say the man hath done unjustly; but we do not seek to be revenged of the fire and of poison, because we cannot make them ask forgiveness, as we would make men to do when they hurt us. So that the blaming of the one and the other, that is, the declaring of the hurt or evil action done by them, is the same in both; but the malice of man is only against man.

(*h*) "No man sins in doing those things which he could not shun."

He may as well say, no man halts which cannot choose but halt; or stumbles, that cannot choose but stumble. For what is sin, but halting or stumbling in the way of God's commandments?

(*i*) "The question then is not, whether a man be necessitated to will or nill, yet free to act or forbear. But, saving the ambiguous acceptions of the word *free*, the question is plainly this," &c.

This question, which the Bishop stateth in this place, I have before set down verbatim and allowed: and it is the same with mine, though he perceive it not. But seeing I did nothing, but at his request set down my opinion, there can be no other question between us in this controversy, but whether my opinion be the truth or not.

(*j*) "So my preface remains yet unanswered. Either I was extrinsically and inevitably predetermined to write this discourse," &c.

That which he saith in the preface is, "that if he be not free to write this discourse, he ought not to be blamed; but if he be free, he hath obtained the cause."

The first consequence I should have granted him, if he had written it rationally and civilly; the latter I deny, and have shown that he ought to have proved that a man is free to will. For that which he says, any thing else whatsoever would think, if it knew it were moved, and did not know what moved it. A wooden top that is lashed by the boys, and runs about sometimes to one wall, sometimes to another, sometimes spinning, sometimes hitting men on the shins, if it were sensible of its own motion, would think it proceeded from its own will, unless it felt what lashed it. And is a man any wiser, when he runs to one place for a benefice, to another for a bargain, and troubles the world with writing errors and requiring answers, because he thinks he doth it without other cause than his own will, and seeth not what are the lashings that cause his will?

II

Determinism

Mill has been chosen as the spokesman of determinism for two reasons. The first is that his determinism is empirical rather than metaphysical or theological, and it is empirical determinism which is most in evidence in contemporary philosophy. His appeal is to observation and statistics, a Libertarian rejoinder to which can be found in chapters VIII and XII of Austin Farrer's *The Freedom of the Will*. The second is the richness of Mill's discussion, which touches upon several points developed by more recent philosophers. Among these are the introspective evidence for free will, the hypothetical analysis of "can," the effort made by the self to act against previously formed character, the retribution theory of punishment, and the distinction between fatalism and determinism. We have omitted a portion of the discussion of punishment and most of Mill's footnotes, which relate his discussion to other thinkers of his time.

The selections by Foot and Taylor present criticisms of assumptions often made by Determinists, and certainly by Mill. Mrs. Foot criticizes the assumption that action for which a person is held responsible must be the causal outcome of motive and character. She asks whether these are causal concepts at all, and suggests alternative interpretations of them. Taylor criticizes the assumption that saying that a person can do something is like saying that a thing has a disposition. He offers an exhaustive analysis of the different uses of the term "can," and although his analysis is a model of the clarity and diligence which would be required in order ever to realize Hume's dream of resolving the free will problem by analysis alone, it is interesting to note that Taylor does not believe that the crucial notion that something is in our power will ever yield to analysis.

From *An Examination of Sir William Hamilton's Philosophy*

JOHN STUART MILL

Sir W. Hamilton having thus, as is often the case (and it is one of the best things he does), saved his opponents the trouble of answering his friends, his doctrine is left resting exclusively on the supports which he has himself provided for it. In examining them, let us place ourselves, in the first instance, completely at his point of view, and concede to him the coequal inconceivability of the conflicting hypotheses, an uncaused commencement, and an infinite regress. But this choice of inconceivabilities is not offered to us in the case of volitions only. We are held, as he not only admits but contends, to the same alternative in all cases of causation whatsoever. But we find our way out of the difficulty, in other cases, in quite a different manner. In the case of every other kind of fact, we do not elect the hypothesis that the event took place without a cause: we accept the other supposition, that of a regress, not indeed to infinity, but either generally into the region of the Unknowable, or back to an Universal Cause, regarding which, as we are only concerned with it in respect of attributes bearing relation to what it preceded, and not as itself preceded by anything, we can afford to consider this reference as ultimate.

Now, what is the reason, which, in the case of all things within the range of our knowledge except volitions, makes us choose this side of the alternative? Why do we, without scruple, register all of them as depending on causes, by which (to use our author's language) they are determined necessarily, though, in believing this, we, according to Sir W. Hamilton, believe as utter an inconceivability as if we supposed them to take place without a cause? Apparently it is because the causation hypothesis, inconceivable as he may think it, possesses the advantage of having experience on its side. And how or by what evidence does experience testify to it? Not by disclosing any *nexus* between the cause and the effect, any Sufficient Reason in the cause itself why the effect should follow it. No philosopher now makes this supposition, and Sir W. Hamil-

From *An Examination of Sir William Hamilton's Philosophy*, Chapter XXVI, "On the Freedom of the Will." (London: Longmans, Green, Reader, and Dyer, 1867.)

ton positively disclaims it. What experience makes known, is the fact of an invariable sequence between every event and some special combination of antecedent conditions, in such sort that wherever and whenever that union of antecedents exists, the event does not fail to occur. Any *must* in the case, any necessity, other than the unconditional universality of the fact, we know nothing of. Still, this à posteriori "does," though not confirmed by an à priori "must," decides our choice between the two inconceivables, and leads us to the belief that every event within the phenomenal universe, except human volitions, is determined to take place by a cause. Now, the so-called Necessitarians demand the application of the same rule of judgment to our volitions. They maintain that there is the same evidence for it. They affirm, as a truth of experience, that volitions do, in point of fact, follow determinate moral antecedents with the same uniformity, and (when we have sufficient knowledge of the circumstances) with the same certainty, as physical effects follow their physical causes. These moral antecedents are desires, aversions, habits, and dispositions, combined with outward circumstances suited to call those internal incentives into action. All these again are effects of causes, those of them which are mental being consequences of education, and of other moral and physical influences. This is what Necessitarians affirm: and they court every possible mode in which its truth can be verified. They test it by each person's observation of his own volitions. They test it by each person's observation of the voluntary actions of those with whom he comes into contact; and by the power which every one has of foreseeing actions, with a degree of exactness proportioned to his previous experience and knowledge of the agents, and with a certainty often quite equal to that with which we predict the commonest physical events. They test it further, by the statistical results of the observation of human beings acting in numbers sufficient to eliminate the influences which operate only on a few, and which on a large scale neutralize one another, leaving the total result about the same as if the volitions of the whole mass had been affected by such only of the determining causes as were common to them all. In cases of this description the results are as uniform, and many may be as accurately foretold, as in any physical inquiries in which the effect depends upon a multiplicity of causes. The cases in which volitions seem too uncertain to admit of being confidently predicted, are those in which our knowledge of the influences antecedently in operation is so incomplete, that with equally imperfect data there would be the same uncertainty in the predictions of the astronomer and the chemist. On these grounds it is contended that our choice between the conflicting inconceivables should be the same in the case of volitions as of all other phenomena; we must reject equally in both cases the hypothesis of spontaneousness, and consider them all as caused. A volition is a moral effect, which follows the corresponding moral causes as certainly and invariably as physical effects follow their physical causes.

Whether it *must* do so, I acknowledge myself to be entirely ignorant, be the phenomenon moral or physical; and I condemn, accordingly, the word Necessity as applied to either case. All I know is, that it always *does.* This argument from experience Sir W. Hamilton passes unnoticed, but urges, on the opposite side of the question, the argument from Consciousness. We are conscious, he affirms, either of our freedom, or at all events (it is odd that, on his theory, there should be any doubt) of something which implies freedom. If this is true, our internal consciousness tells us that we have a power, which the whole outward experience of the human race tells us that we never use. This is surely a very unfortunate predicament we are in, and a sore trial to the puzzled metaphysician. Philosophy is far from having so easy a business before her as our author thinks: the arbiter Consciousness is by no means invoked to turn the scale between two equally balanced difficulties; on the contrary, she has to sit in judgment between herself and a complete induction from experience. Consciousness, it will probably be said, is the best evidence; and so it would be, if we were always certain what is Consciousness. . . .

Let us cross-examine the alleged testimony of consciousness. And, first, it is left in some uncertainty by Sir W. Hamilton whether Consciousness makes only one deliverance on the subject, or two: whether we are conscious only of moral responsibility, in which free-will is implied, or are directly conscious of free-will. In his Lectures, Sir W. Hamilton speaks only of the first. In the notes on Reid, which were written subsequently, he seems to affirm both, but the latter of the two in a doubtful and hesitating manner: so difficult, in reality, does he find it to ascertain with certainty what it is that Consciousness certifies. But as there are many who maintain with a confidence far greater than his, that we are directly conscious of free-will, it is necessary to examine that question.

To be conscious of free-will, must mean, to be conscious, before I have decided, that I am able to decide either way. Exception may be taken *in limine* to the use of the word consciousness in such an application. Consciousness tells me what I do or feel. But what I am *able* to do, is not a subject of consciousness. Consciousness is not prophetic; we are conscious of what is, not of what will or can be. We never know that we are able to do a thing, except from having done it, or something equal and similar to it. We should not know that we were capable of action at all, if we had never acted. Having acted, we know, as far as that experience reaches, how we are able to act; and this knowledge, when it has become familiar, is often confounded with, and called by the name of, consciousness. But it does not derive any increase of authority from being misnamed; its truth is not supreme over, but depends on, experience. If our so-called consciousness of what we are able to do is not borne out by experience, it is a delusion. It has not title to credence but as an interpretation of experience, and if it is a false interpretation, it must give way.

But this conviction, whether termed consciousness or only belief, that our will is free—what is it? Of what are we convinced? I am told that whether I decide to do or to abstain, I feel that I could have decided the other way. I ask my consciousness what I do feel, and I find, indeed, that I feel (or am convinced) that I could, and even should, have chosen the other course if I had preferred it, that is, if I had liked it better; but not that I could have chosen one course while I preferred the other. When I say preferred, I of course include with the thing itself, all that accompanies it. I know that I can, because I know that I often do, elect to do one thing, when I should have preferred another in itself, apart from its consequences, or from a moral law which it violates. And this preference for a thing in itself, abstractedly from its accompaniments, is often loosely described as preference for the thing. It is this unprecise mode of speech which makes it not seem absurd to say that I act in opposition to my preference; that I do one thing when I would rather do another; that my conscience prevails over my desires—as if conscience were not itself a desire—the desire to do right. Take any alternative: say to murder or not to murder. I am told, that if I elect to murder, I am conscious that I could have elected to abstain: but am I conscious that I could have abstained if my aversion to the crime, and my dread of its consequences, had been weaker than the temptation? If I elect to abstain: in what sense am I conscious that I could have elected to commit the crime? Only if I had desired to commit it with a desire stronger than my horror of murder; not with one less strong. When we think of ourselves hypothetically as having acted otherwise than we did, we always suppose a difference in the antecedents: we picture ourselves as having known something that we did not know, or not known something that we did know; which is a difference in the external inducements; or as having desired something, or disliked something, more or less than we did; which is a difference in the internal inducements.

In refutation of this it is said, that in resisting a desire, I am conscious of making an effort; that after I have resisted, I have the remembrance of having made an effort; that "if the temptation was long continued, or if I have been resisting the strong will of another, I am as sensibly exhausted by that effort, as after any physical exertion I ever made:" and it is added, "If my volition is wholly determined by the strongest present desire, it will be decided without any effort. . . . When the greater weight goes down, and the lesser up, no effort is needed on the part of the scales." [1] It is implied in this argument, that in a battle between contrary impulses, the victory must always be decided in a moment; that the force which is really the strongest, and prevails ultimately, must prevail instantaneously. The fact is not quite thus even in inanimate nature: the hurricane does not level the house or blow down the tree with-

---

[1] The Battle of the Two Philosophies, pp. 13, 14.

out resistance; even the balance trembles, and the scales oscillate for a short time, when the difference of the weights is not considerable. Far less does victory come without a contest to the strongest of two moral, or even two vital forces, whose nature it is to be never fixed, but always flowing, quantities. In a struggle between passions, there is not a single instant in which there does not pass across the mind some thought, which adds strength to, or takes it from, one or the other of the contending powers. Unless one of them was, from the beginning, out of all proportion stronger than the other, some time must elapse before the balance adjusts itself between forces neither of which is for any two successive instants the same. During that interval the agent is in the peculiar mental and physical state which we call a conflict of feelings: and we all know that a conflict between strong feelings *is*, in an extraordinary degree, exhaustive of the nervous energies.[2] The consciousness of effort, which we are told of, is this state of conflict. The author I am quoting considers what he calls, I think improperly, an effort, to be only on one side, because he represents to himself the conflict as taking place between me and some foreign power, which I conquer, or by which I am overcome. But it is obvious that "I" am both parties in the contest; the conflict is between me and myself; between (for instance) me desiring a pleasure, and me dreading self-reproach. What causes Me, or, if you please, my Will, to be identified with one side rather than with the other, is that one of the Me's represents a more permanent state of my feelings than the other does. After the temptation has been yielded to, the desiring "I" will come to an end, but the conscience-stricken "I" may endure to the end of life.

I therefore dispute altogether that we are conscious of being able to act in opposition to the strongest present desire or aversion. The difference between a bad and a good man is not that the latter acts on opposition to his strongest desire; it is that his desire to do right, and his aversion to doing wrong, are strong enough to overcome, and in the case of perfect virtue, to silence, any other desire or aversion which may conflict with them. It is because this state of mind is possible to human nature, that human beings are capable of moral government: and moral education consists in subjecting them to the discipline which has most tendency to bring them into this state. The object of moral education is to educate the will: but the will can only be educated through the desires and aversions; by eradicating or weakening such of them as are likeliest to lead to evil; exalting to the highest pitch the desire of right conduct and the aversion to wrong; cultivating all other desires and aversions of

---

[2] The writer I quote says, "Balancing one motive against another is not willing but judging." The state of mind I am speaking of is by no means a state of judging. It is an emotional, not an intellectual state, and the judging may be finished before it commences. If there were any indispensable act of judging in this stage, it could only be judging which of the two pains or pleasures was the greatest: and to regard this as the operative force would be conceding the point in favor of Necessitarianism.

which the ordinary operation is auxiliary to right, while discountenancing so immoderate an indulgence of them, as might render them too powerful to be overcome by the moral sentiment, when they chance to be in opposition to it. The other requisites are, a clear intellectual standard of right and wrong, that moral desire and aversion may act in the proper places, and such general mental habits as shall prevent moral considerations from being forgotten or overlooked, in cases to which they are rightly applicable.

Rejecting, then, the figment of a direct consciousness of the freedom of the will, in other words, our ability to will in opposition to our strongest preference; it remains to consider whether, as affirmed by Sir W. Hamilton, a freedom of this kind is implied in what is called our consciousness of moral responsibility. There must be something very plausible in this opinion, since it is shared even by Necessitarians. Many of these—in particular Mr. Owen and his followers—from a recognition of the fact that volitions are effects of causes, have been led to deny human responsibility. I do not mean that they denied moral distinctions. Few persons have had a stronger sense of right and wrong, or been more devoted to the things they deemed right. What they denied was the rightfulness of inflicting punishment. A man's actions, they said, are the result of his character, and he is not the author of his own character. It is made *for* him, not *by* him. There is no justice in punishing him for what he cannot help. We should try to convince or persuade him that he had better act in a different manner; and should educate all, especially the young, in the habits and dispositions which lead to well-doing: though how this is to be effected without any use whatever of punishment as a means of education, is a question they have failed to resolve. The confusion of ideas, which make the subjection of human volitions to the law of Causation seem inconsistent with accountability, must thus be very natural to the human mind; but this may be said of a thousand errors, and even of some merely verbal fallacies. In the present case there is more than a verbal fallacy, but verbal fallacies also contribute their part.

What is meant by moral responsibility? Responsibility means punishment. When we are said to have the feeling of being morally responsible for our actions, the idea of being punished for them is uppermost in the speaker's mind. But the feeling of liability to punishment is of two kinds. It may mean, expectation that if we act in a certain manner, punishment will actually be inflicted upon us, by our fellow creatures or by a Supreme Power. Or it may only mean, knowing that we shall deserve that infliction.

The first of these cannot, in any correct meaning of the term, be designated as a consciousness. If we believe that we shall be punished for doing wrong, it is because the belief has been taught to us by our parents and tutors, or by our religion, or is generally held by those who surround us, or because we have ourselves come to the conclusion by reasoning, or from the experience of life. This is not Consciousness. And, by whatever name it is called, its evidence is not dependent on any theory of the spontaneousness of volition. The punishment of guilt in another world is believed with undoubting conviction by Turkish fatalists, and by professed Christians who are not only Necessitarians, but believe that the majority of mankind were divinely predestined from all eternity to sin and to be punished for sinning. It is not, therefore, the belief that we shall be *made* accountable, which can be deemed to require or presuppose the free-will hypothesis; it is the belief that we ought so to be; that we are justly accountable; that guilt deserves punishment. It is here that issue is joined between the two opinions. . . .

The real question is one of justice—the legitimacy of retribution, or punishment. On the theory of Necessity (we are told) a man cannot help acting as he does; and it cannot be just that he should be punished for what he cannot help.

Not if the expectation of punishment enables him to help it, and is the only means by which he can be enabled to help it?

To say that he cannot help it, is true or false, according to the qualification with which the assertion is accompanied. Supposing him to be of a vicious disposition, he cannot help doing the criminal act, if he is allowed to believe that he will be able to commit it unpunished. If, on the contrary, the impression is strong in his mind that a heavy punishment will follow, he can, and in most cases does, help it.

The question deemed to be so puzzling is, how punishment can be justified, if men's actions are determined by motives, among which motives punishment is one. A more difficult question would be, how it can be justified if they are not so determined. Punishment proceeds on the assumption that the will is governed by motives. If punishment had no power of acting on the will, it would be illegitimate, however natural might be the inclination to inflict it. Just so far as the will is supposed free, that is, capable of acting *against* motives, punishment is disappointed of its object, and deprived of its justification.

There are two ends which, on the Necessitarian theory, are sufficient to justify punishment: the benefit of the offender himself, and the protection of others. The first justifies it, because to benefit a person cannot be to do him an injury. To punish him for his own good, provided the inflictor has any proper title to constitute himself a judge, is no more unjust than to administer medicine. As far, indeed, as respects the criminal himself, the theory of punishment is, that by counterbalancing the influence of present temptations, or acquired bad habits, it restores the mind to that normal preponderance of the love of right, which many moralists and theologians consider to constitute the true definition of our freedom. In its other aspect, punishment is a precaution taken by society in self-defence. To make this just, the only condition required is, that the end which society is attempting to enforce by punishment, should be a just one. Used as a means of aggression by society on the just rights of the individual, punishment is unjust. Used to protect the just rights of others against unjust aggression by the offender, it is just. If it is possible to have just rights, (which is the same thing as to have rights at all) it cannot be unjust to defend them. Free-will or no free-will, it is just to punish so far as is necessary for this purpose, as it is just to put a wild beast to death (without unnecessary suffering) for the same object. . . .

If, indeed, punishment is inflicted for any other reason than in order to operate on the will; if its purpose be other than that of improving the culprit himself, or securing the just rights of others against unjust violation, then, I admit, the case is totally altered. If any one thinks that there is justice in the infliction of purposeless suffering; that there is a natural affinity between the two ideas of guilt and punishment, which makes it intrinsically fitting that wherever there has been guilt, pain should be inflicted by way of retribution; I acknowledge that I can find no argument to justify punishment inflicted on this principle. As a legitimate satisfaction to feelings of indignation and resentment which are on the whole salutary and worthy of cultivation, I can in certain cases admit it; but here it is still a means to an end. The merely retributive view of punishment derives no justification from the doctrine I support. But it derives quite as little from the free-will doctrine. Suppose it true that the will of a malefactor, when he committed an offence, was free, or in other words, that he acted badly, not because he was of a bad disposition, but from no cause in particular: it is not easy to deduce from this the conclusion that it is just to punish him. That his acts were beyond the command of motives might be a good reason for keeping out of his way, or placing him under bodily restraint; but no reason for inflicting pain upon him, when that pain, by supposition, could not operate as a deterring motive.

While the doctrine I advocate does not support the idea that punishment in mere retaliation is justifiable, it at the same time fully accounts for the general and natural sentiment of its being so. From our earliest childhood, the idea of doing wrong (that is, of doing what is forbidden, or what is injurious to others) and the idea of punishment are presented to our mind together, and the intense character of the impressions causes the association between them to attain the highest degree of closeness and intimacy. Is it strange, or unlike the usual processes of the human mind, that in these circumstances we should retain the feeling, and forget the reason on which it is grounded? But why do I speak of forgetting? In most cases the reason has never, in our early education, been presented to the mind. The only ideas presented have been those of wrong and punishment, and an inseparable association has been created between these directly, without the help of any intervening idea. This is quite enough to make the spontaneous feelings of mankind regard punishment and a wrongdoer as naturally fitted to each other—as a conjunction appropriate in itself, independently of any consequences. . . .

That a person holding what is called the Necessitarian doctrine should on that account *feel* that it would be unjust to punish him for his wrong actions, seems to me the veriest of chimeras. Yes, if he really "could not help" acting as he did, that is, if it did not depend on his will; if he was under physical constraint, or even if he was under the action of such a violent motive that no fear of punishment could have any effect; which, if capable of being ascertained, is a just ground of exemption, and is the reason why by the laws of most countries people are not punished for what they were compelled to do by immediate danger of death. But if the criminal was in a state capable of being operated upon by the fear of punishment, no metaphysical objection, I believe, will make him feel his punishment unjust. Neither will he feel that because his act was the consequence of motives, operating upon a certain mental disposition, it was not his own fault. For, first, it was at all events his own defect or infirmity, for which the expectation of punishment is the appropriate cure. And secondly, the word fault, so far from being inapplicable, is the specific name for the kind of defect or infirmity which he has displayed—insufficient love of good and aversion to evil. The weakness of these feelings or their strength is in every one's mind the standard of fault or merit, of degrees of fault and degrees of merit. Whether we are judging of particular actions, or of the character of a person, we are wholly guided by the indications afforded of the energy of these influences. If the desire of right and aversion to wrong have yielded to a small temptation, we judge them to be weak, and our disapprobation is strong. If the temptation to which they have yielded is so great that even strong feelings of virtue might have succumbed to it, our moral reprobation is less intense. If, again, the moral desires and aversions have prevailed, but not over a very strong force, we hold the action was good, but that there was little merit in it; and our estimate of the merit rises, in exact proportion to the greatness of the obstacle which the moral feeling proved strong enough to overcome.

Mr. Mansel [3] has furnished what he thinks a refutation of the Necessitarian argument, of which it is well to take notice, the more so, perhaps, as it is directed against some remarks on the subject by the present writer in a former work[4] remarks which were not intended as an argument for so-called Necessity, but only to place the nature and meaning of that ill-understood doctrine in a truer light. With this purpose in view, it was remarked that "by saying that a man's actions necessarily follow from his character, all that is really meant (for no more is meant in any case

[3] Prolegomena Logica, Note C at the end.
[4] System of Logic, Book vi. ch. 2.

whatever of causation) is that he invariably does act in conformity to his character, and that any one who thoroughly knew his character, could certainly predict how he would act in any supposable case. No more than this is contended for by any one but an Asiatic fatalist." "And no more than this," observes Mr. Mansel, "is needed to construct a system of fatalism as rigid as any Asiatic can desire."

Mr. Mansel is mistaken in thinking that the doctrine of the causation of human actions is fatalism at all, or resembles fatalism in any of its moral or intellectual effects. To call it by that name is to break down a fundamental distinction. Real fatalism is of two kinds. Pure, or Asiatic fatalism,—the fatalism of the Œdipus,—holds that our actions do not depend upon our desires. Whatever our wishes may be, a superior power, or an abstract destiny, will overrule them, and compel us to act, not as we desire, but in the manner predestined. Our love of good and hatred of evil are of no efficacy, and though in themselves they may be virtuous, as far as conduct is concerned it is unavailing to cultivate them. The other kind, Modified Fatalism I will call it, holds that our actions are determined by our will, our will by our desires, and our desires by the joint influence of the motives presented to us and of our individual character; but that, our character having been made for us and not by us, we are not responsible for it, nor for the actions it leads to, and should in vain attempt to alter them. The true doctrine of the Causation of human actions maintains, in opposition to both, that not only our conduct, but our character, is in part amenable to our will; that we can, by employing the proper means, improve our character; and that if our character is such that while it remains what it is, it necessitates us to do wrong, it will be just to apply motives which will necessitate us to strive for its improvement, and so emancipate ourselves from the other necessity. In other words, we are under a moral obligation to seek the improvement of our moral character. We shall not indeed do so unless we desire our improvement, and desire it more than we dislike the means which must be employed for the purpose. But does Mr. Mansel, or any other of the free-will philosophers think that we can will the means if we do not desire the end, or if our desire of the end is weaker than our aversion to the means?

Mr. Mansel is more rigid in his ideas of what the free-will theory requires, than one of the most eminent of the thinkers who have adopted it. According to Mr. Mansel, the belief that whoever knew perfectly our character and our circumstances could predict our actions, amounts to Asiatic fatalism. According to Kant, in his Metaphysics of Ethics, such capability of prediction is quite compatible with the freedom of the will. This seems, at first sight, to be an admission of everything which the rational supporters of the opposite theory could desire. But Kant avoids this consequence, by changing (as lawyers would say) the *venue* of free-will, from our actions generally, to the formation of our character. It is in that, he thinks, we are free, and he is almost willing to admit that while our character is what it is, our actions are necessitated by it. In drawing this distinction, the philosopher of Königsberg saves inconvenient facts at the expense of the consistency of his theory. There cannot be one theory for one kind of voluntary actions, and another theory for the other kinds. When we voluntarily exert ourselves, as it is our duty to do, for the improvement of our character, or when we act in a manner which (either consciously on our part or unconsciously) deteriorates it, these, like all other voluntary acts, presuppose that there was already something in our character, or in that combined with our circumstances, which led us to do so, and accounts for our doing so. The person, therefore, who is supposed able to predict our actions from our character as it now is, would, under the same conditions of perfect knowledge, be equally able to predict what we should do to change our character: and if this be the meaning of necessity, that part of our conduct is as necessary as all the rest. If necessity means more than this abstract possibility of being foreseen; if it means any mysterious compulsion, apart from simple invariability of sequence, I deny it as strenuously as any one in the case of human volitions, but I deny it just as much of all other phenomena. To enforce this distinction was the principal object of the remarks which Mr. Mansel has criticized. If an unessential distinction from Mr. Mansel's point of view, it is essential from mine, and of supreme importance in a practical aspect.

The free-will metaphysicians have made little endeavour to prove that we can will in opposition to our strongest desire, but have strenuously maintained that we can will when we have no strongest desire. With this view Dr. Reid formerly, and Mr. Mansel now, have thrown in the teeth of Necessitarians the famous *asinus Buridani*. If, say they, the will were solely determined by motives, the ass, between two bundles of hay exactly alike, and equally distant from him, would remain undecided until he died of hunger. From Sir W. Hamilton's notes on this chapter of Reid, I infer that he did not countenance this argument; and it is surprising that writers of talent should have seen anything in it. I wave the objection that if it applies at all, it proves that the ass also has free-will; for perhaps he has. But the ass, it is affirmed, would starve before he decided. Yes, possibly, if he remained all the time in a fixed attitude of deliberation; if he never for an instant ceased to balance one against another the rival attractions, and if they really were so exactly equal that no dwelling on them could detect any difference. But this is not the way in which things take place on our planet. From mere lassitude, if from no other cause, he would intermit the process, and cease thinking of the rival objects at all: until a moment arrived when he would be seeing or thinking of one only, and that fact, combined with the sensation of hunger, would determine him to a decision.

But the argument on which Mr. Mansel lays most stress (it is also one of Reid's) is the following. Necessitarians say that the will is governed by the strongest motive: "but I only know the strength of motives in relation to the will by the test of ultimate prevalence; so that this means no more than that the prevailing motive prevails." I have heretofore complimented Mr. Mansel on seeing farther, in some things, than his master. In the present instance I am compelled to remark, that he has not seen so far. Sir W. Hamilton was not the man to neglect an argument like this, had there been no flaw in it. The fact is that there are two. First, those who say that the will follows the strongest motive, do not mean the motive which is strongest in relation to the will, or in other words, that the will follows what it does follow. They mean the motive which is strongest in relation to pain and pleasure; since a motive, being a desire or aversion, is proportional to the pleasantness, as conceived by us, of the thing desired, or the painfulness of the thing shunned. And when what was at first a direct impulse towards pleasure, or recoil from pain, has passed into a habit or a fixed purpose, then the strength of the motive means the completeness and promptitude of the association which has been formed between an idea and an outward act. This is the first answer to Mr. Mansel. The second is, that even supposing there were no test of the strength of motives but their effect on the will, the proposition that the will follows the strongest motive would not, as Mr. Mansel supposes, be identical and unmeaning. We say, without absurdity, that if two weights are placed in opposite scales, the heavier will lift the other up; yet we mean nothing by the heavier, except the weight which will lift up the other. The proposition, nevertheless, is not unmeaning, for it signifies that in many or most cases there *is* a heavier, and that this is always the same one, not one or the other as it may happen. In like manner, even if the strongest motive meant only the motive which prevails, yet if there is a prevailing motive—if, all other antecedents being the same, the motive which prevails to-day will prevail to-morrow and every subsequent day—Sir W. Hamilton was acute enough to see that the free-will theory is not saved. I regret that I cannot, in this instance, credit Mr. Mansel with the same acuteness.

Before leaving the subject, it is worth while to remark, that not only the doctrine of Necessity, but Predestination in its coarsest form—the belief that all our actions are divinely preordained—though, in my view, inconsistent with ascribing any moral attributes whatever to the Deity, yet if combined with the belief that God works according to general laws, which have to be learnt from experience, has no tendency to make us act in any respect otherwise than we should do if we thought our actions really contingent. For if God acts according to general laws, then, whatever he may have preordained, he has preordained that it shall take place through the causes on which experience shows it to be consequent: and if he has predestined that I shall attain my ends, he has predestined that I shall do so by studying and putting in practice the means which lead

eir attainment. When the belief in predestination has a paralysing
ct on conduct, as is sometimes the case with Mahometans, it is be-
use they fancy they can infer what God has predestined, without wait-
ing for the result. They think that either by particular signs of some
sort, or from the general aspect of things, they can perceive the issue
towards which God is working, and having discovered this, naturally
deem useless any attempt to defeat it. Because something will certainly
happen if nothing is done to prevent it, they think it will certainly happen whatever may be done to prevent it; in a word, they believe in Necessity in the only proper meaning of the term—an issue unalterable by
human efforts or desires.

Free Will as Involving Determinism

PHILIPPA FOOT

The idea that free will can be reconciled with the strictest determinism is now very widely accepted. To say that a man acted freely is, it is often suggested, to say that he was not constrained, or that he could have done otherwise if he had chosen, or something else of that kind; and since these things could be true even if his action was determined it seems that there could be room for free will even within a universe completely subject to causal laws. Hume put forward a view of this kind in contrasting the "liberty of spontaneity . . . which is oppos'd to violence" with the nonexistent "liberty of indifference . . . which means a negation of necessity and causes." [1] A. J. Ayer, in his essay "Freedom and Necessity" [2] was summing up such a position when he said, "from the fact that my action is causally determined . . . it does not necessarily follow that I am not free" [3] and "it is not when my action has any cause at all, but only when it has a special sort of cause, that it is reckoned not to be free." [4]

I am not here concerned with the merits of this view but only with a theory which appears more or less incidentally in the writings of those who defend it. This is the argument that so far from being incompatible with determinism, free will actually requires it. It appears briefly in Hume's *Treatise* and was set out in full in an article by R. E. Hobart.[5] P. H. Nowell-Smith was expressing a similar view when he said of the idea that determinism is opposed to free will that "the clearest proof that it is mistaken or at least muddled lies in showing that I could not be free to choose what I do *unless* determinism is correct. . . . Freedom, so far from being incompatible with causality implies it." [6] Ayer has taken

"Free Will as Involving Determinism," *The Philosophical Review*, LXVI (1957), pp. 439-450. Reprinted by permission.

[1] *Treatise*, bk. II, pt. III, sec. 2.
[2] *Polemic,* no. 5 (1946); reprinted in his *Philosophical Essays* (London, 1954).
[3] *Philosophical Essays,* p. 278.
[4] *Ibid.,* p. 281.
[5] "Freewill as Involving Determinism," *Mind*, XLIII (1934), 1-27.
[6] "Freewill and Moral Responsibility," *Mind*, LVII (1948), 46.

up a similar position, arguing that the absence of causal laws governing action "does not give the moralist what he wants. For he is anxious to show that men are capable of acting freely in order to infer that they can be morally responsible for what they do. But if it is a matter of pure chance that a man should act in one way rather than another, he may be free but he can hardly be responsible." [7]

This argument is not essential to the main thesis of those who use it; their own account of free will in such terms as the absence of *constraining* causes might be correct even though there were no inconsistencies in the suggestion put forward by their libertarian opponents. But if valid the argument would be a strong argument, disposing of the position of anyone who argued both that free will required the absence of determining causes and that free will was a possibility. That the argument is not valid, and indeed that it is singularly implausible, I shall now try to show. It is, I think, surprising that it should have survived so long: this is perhaps because it has not had to bear much weight. In any case the weapons which can be used against it are ones which are in general use elsewhere.

In discussing determinism and free will it is important to be clear about the sense which is given in this context to words such as "determined" and "caused." Russell gave this account:

> The law of universal causation . . . may be enunciated as follows. There are such invariable relations between different events at the same or different times that, given the state of the whole universe throughout any finite time, however short, every previous and subsequent event can theoretically be determined as a function of the given events during that time. [8]

This seems to be the kind of determinism which worries the defender of free will, for if human action is subject to a universal law of causation of this type, there will be for any action a set of sufficient conditions which can be traced back to factors outside the control of the agent.

We cannot of course take it for granted that whenever the word "determined" or the word "cause" is used this is what is implied, and what is intended may be in no way relevant to the question of free will. For instance, an action said to be determined by the desires of the man who does it is not necessarily an action for which there is supposed to be a sufficient condition. In saying that it is determined by his desires we may mean merely that he is doing something that he wants to do, or that he is doing it for the sake of something else that he wants. There is nothing in this to suggest determinism in Russell's sense. On the whole it is wise

---

[7] *Philosophical Essays*, p. 275.

[8] "On the Notion of Cause," in *Our Knowledge of the External World* (London, 1914), p. 221.

to be suspicious of expressions such as "determined by desire" unless these have been given a clear sense, and this is particularly true of the phrase "determined by the agent's character." Philosophers often talk about actions being determined by a man's character, but it is not certain that anyone else does, or that the words are given any definite sense. One might suppose that an action was so determined if it was *in* character, for instance the generous action of a generous man; but if this is so we will not have the kind of determinism traditionally supposed to raise difficulties for a doctrine of free will. For nothing has been said to suggest that where the character trait can be predicated the action will invariably follow; it has not been supposed that a man who can truly be said to be generous never acts ungenerously even under given conditions.

Keeping the relevant sense of "determinism" in mind, we may now start to discuss the view that free will requires determinism. The first version which I shall consider is that put forward by Hobart, who suggests that an action which is not determined cannot properly be called an *action* at all, being something that happened to the agent rather than something he *did*. Hobart says, *"In proportion* as it (the action) is undetermined, it is just as if his legs should suddenly spring up and carry him off where he did not prefer to go." To see how odd this suggestion is we have only to ask when we would say that a man's legs were carrying him where he did not prefer to go. One can imagine the scene: he is sitting quietly in his chair and has said that he is going to go on reading his book; suddenly he cries, "Good heavens, I can't control my legs!" and as he moves across the room, he hangs on to the furniture or asks someone else to hold him. Here indeed his legs are carrying him where he does not want to go, but what has this to do with indeterminism, and what has the ordinary case, where he walks across the room, to do with determinism? Perhaps Hobart thinks that when a man does something meaning to do it, he does what he wants to do, and so his action is determined by his desire. But to do something meaning to do it is to do it in a certain way, not to do it as the result of the operation of a causal law. When one means to do something, one does not call out for help in preventing the movement of one's limbs; on the contrary, one is likely to stop other people from interfering, saying, "I want to do this." It is by such factors that walking across the room is distinguished from being carried off by one's legs. It is to be explained in terms of the things said and done by the agent, not in terms of some force, "the desire," present before the action was done and still less in terms of some law telling us that whenever this "desire" is found it will be followed by the action. The indeterminist has no difficulty in distinguishing an action from something that happens to the agent; he can say exactly the same as anyone else.

Nowell-Smith seems to be thinking along somewhat the same lines as

Hobart when he attacks C. A. Campbell for saying that free will requires indeterminism:

> The essence of Campbell's account is that the action should not be predictable from a knowledge of the agent's character. But, if this is so, can what he does be called *his* action at all? Is it not rather a *lusus naturae,* an Act of God or a miracle? If a hardened criminal, bent on robbing the poorbox, suddenly and *inexplicably* fails to do so, we should not say that he *chose* to resist or deserves *credit* for resisting the temptation; we should say, if we were religious, that he was the recipient of a sudden outpouring of Divine Grace or, if we were irreligious, that his "action" was due to chance, which is another way of saying that it was inexplicable. In either case we should refuse to use the active voice.[9]

It is hard to see why a man who does something inexplicably does not really *do* it. Let us suppose that the hardened criminal's action really is inexplicable; we can only say, "He just turned away," and not why he did so; this does not mean that he did it by accident, or unintentionally, or not of his own free will, I see no reason for refusing to use the active voice. In any case, to explain an action is not necessarily to show that it could have been predicted from some fact about the agent's character—that he is weak, greedy, sentimental, and so forth. We may if we like say that an action is never *fully* explained unless it has been shown to be covered by a law which connects it to such a character trait; but then it becomes even more implausible to say that an action must be explicable if we are to admit it as something genuinely *done*. In the ordinary sense we explain the criminal's action if we say, for instance, that a particular thought came into his mind; we do not also have to find a law about the way such thoughts do come into the minds of such men.

A rather different version of this argument runs as follows. We hold responsible only a man who is a rational agent; if someone were always to do things out of the blue, without having any reason to do them, we should be inclined to count him as a lunatic, one who could not be held responsible for his actions, so that even if he *did* things he would do things for which he could not be held responsible. And is it not through being determined by motives that actions are those of a rational agent whom we can praise or blame?

It certainly would be odd to suppose that free will required the absence of motives for action. We do not of course expect that everything that the rational man does should be done with a motive; if he gets up and walks about the room he need not be doing so in order to take exercise; it is quite usual for people to do this kind of thing without any particular purpose in view, and no one is counted irrational for doing so. And yet we do expect a man to have a motive for a great number of the things

[9] *Ethics* (London, 1954), pp. 281-282.

that he does, and we would count anyone who constantly performed troublesome actions without a motive as irrational. So it looks as if a moral agent is a man whose actions are in general determined, if determinism is involved in "having a motive" for what he does.

What does it mean to say that someone had a motive for doing what he did? Often this particular expression means that he did it with a particular intention, so we should first say something about intentions and the sense in which they can be said to determine action. We say that a man had a certain intention in acting when he aimed at a certain thing, and "his motive for such and such" often means "his aim in doing such and such," for instance, "His motive for going to the station was to take a train to London." But where motives are intentions it is clear that they cannot be determining causes; for intending to do x and being ready to take the steps thought necessary to do x are connected not empirically but analytically. A man cannot be said to have an intention unless he is reconciled to what he believes to be the intermediate steps. We cannot speak as if the intention were something which could be determined first, and "being ready to take the necessary steps" were a second stage following on the first.

It might be objected that this does not cover the case of "doing y because one wants x" where "wanting x" does not imply trying to get x. In one sense of "want" it is possible to say, "He wants x" without knowing whether he is prepared to take steps to get it. (One might, for instance, want to go to London but not be prepared to spend the money to get there.) So that *wanting* seems here to be a separate condition, which might in certain cases be connected by an empirical law to the adoption of particular courses of action. Certainly wanting is not an event, but one gets rid of wanting as a determining factor too easily if one merely says that desires are not causes because they are not occurrences.

We say "He wants" in this sense where he would adopt certain policies *if* there were no reasons for not doing so. We can say, "He wants to get to London," even when he is not prepared to take the necessary steps to get to London, provided he can say "Trains are too expensive," or "Hitchhiking is too uncomfortable." If we offered him a spare railway ticket or otherwise disposed of his reasons against going, and he still did not go, we would have to say, "He didn't really want to go after all." So wanting in this sense is being prepared to act under certain conditions, though not being prepared to act under the given conditions. It is a description which could be applied to a man before we knew whether he was ready to act in a given situation, and it seems that there might then be a causal relation between the wanting and the acting where the latter took place. This is quite true; there could be a law to the effect that when the description "He wants x" applied at t_1, the description "He is taking the necessary steps to get x" applied at t_2. It would be possible to say this without making a mistake about what it is to *want* and inventing a hidden condition of body or mind. One could say, "Wanting in this sense just is being prepared to act under some conditions," and still maintain that there could be an empirical law connecting wanting with acting under a particular set of conditions. The mistake lies not in the idea that such laws are *possible* but in the thought that there is a reference to them in the statement that a man did one thing because he wanted something else.

So far we have been dealing only with cases in which a question about a motive was answered by specifying something aimed at or wanted. Now we should turn to the cases in which the motive is said to be kindness, vanity, ambition, meanness, jealousy, and so on, to see whether determinism is involved.

It is easy to show that a motive is not a cause in Russell's sense, for it is clearly not an antecedent cause. Professor Gilbert Ryle has pointed out that a man who acts out of vanity is not a man who had a feeling of vanity immediately before he acted, and if it is objected that the vanity which preceded the action need not have manifested itself in a feeling, one may ask what else *would* count as the vanity which was causing him to act. A man's motives are not given by what was happening to him immediately before he started to act. Nor do we discover some independent condition contemporaneous with the action and a law linking the two, for again there is nothing which would count as vanity except the tendency to do this kind of thing.

So much is implied in what Ryle says about acting out of vanity, but his own account of what it is to do so still uses something which is objectionably like a causal model. The analogy which he thinks apt is that between saying a man acted out of vanity and saying a piece of glass broke because it was brittle: "To explain an act as done from a certain motive is not analogous to saying that the glass broke because a stone hit it, but to the quite different type of statement that the glass broke, when the stone hit it, because the glass was brittle." [10] The positive part of this statement seems to me mistaken. Acting out of vanity is not so closely connected with being vain as Ryle must suppose it to be. Let us suppose that his account of what it is to be vain is entirely correct; to say that a man is vain is to say that he tends to behave in certain ways, to feel aggrieved in particular situations, and so on.[11] It does not follow that ascribing vanity as a motive for an action is bringing this action under the "lawlike" proposition that the agent is a man who tends to do these things. For it makes sense to say that a man acts out of vanity on a particular occasion although he is not in general vain, or even vain about this kind of thing. It cannot therefore be true that when we speak of an agent's motive for a particular action we are explaining it in terms of his character, as Ryle suggests; we are not saying "he *would* do that." It is

[10] *Concept of Mind* (London, 1949), pp. 86-87.
[11] *Ibid.*, p. 86.

of course possible to give a motive and to say that the agent has the character trait concerned, but the latter cannot be included in an account of what it is to assign a motive to a particular action.

The explanation of why Ryle says what he does seems to lie in the fact that he has taken a false example of explaining an action by giving a motive. He considers as his example the explanation, "He boasted because he is vain," which is not in fact an explanation of the right type; considered as a statement assigning a motive to a particular action it would be uninformative, for except in very special cases *boasting* is acting out of vanity. It is not surprising that this particular sentence has a different function—that of relating this act of vanity to the character trait. What Ryle says about the example is correct, but it is not an example of the kind of thing he is trying to describe.

It might seem as if we could reformulate the theory to meet the objection about the man who acts out of vanity on one occasion by saying that a man's acting out of vanity is like glass breaking because of a brittleness which could be temporary. "He acted out of vanity" would then be explained as meaning that at that particular time he tended to react in the ways described by Ryle. (If he finds a chance of securing the admiration and envy of others, he does whatever he thinks will produce this admiration and envy.) This is wrong because, whereas glass which is even temporarily brittle has all the reactions which go by this name, a man who is temporarily acting out of vanity is not liable to do other things of this kind. To find concepts which this model would fit one must turn to such descriptions as "a boastful mood," "a savage frame of mind," or "a fit of bad temper."

Assigning a motive to an action is not bringing it under any law; it is rather saying something about the kind of action it was, the direction in which it was tending, or what it was done *as*. A possible comparison would be with the explanation of a movement in a dance which consisted in saying what was being danced. Often in diagnosing motives we should look to purposes—to what the action was done for. This we should discover if we found out what the agent was prepared to go without and what he insisted on having; the fact that visitors are made to admire a garden even in the rain is strong evidence that they were invited out of vanity rather than kindness. In other cases finding the motive will be better described as finding what was being done—finding, for instance, that someone was *taking revenge*. We should take it that a man's motive was revenge if we discovered that he was intentionally harming someone and that his doing so was conditional on his believing that that person has injured him. In the same way we should take it that someone was acting out of gratitude if he (1) intended to confer a benefit and (2) saw this as called for by a past kindness. The fact that it is only the character of the particular action which is involved shows how far we are from anything which could involve motives as determining causes.

We have now considered two suggestions: (1) that an undetermined action would not be one which could properly be attributed to an agent as something that he *did* and (2) that an undetermined action would not be the action of a *rational* agent. A third version, the one put forward by Hume, suggests that an undetermined action would be one for which it would be impossible to praise or blame, punish or reward a man, because it would be connected with nothing permanent in his nature.

> 'Tis only (Hume says) upon the principles of necessity, that a person acquires any merit or demerit from his actions. . . . Actions are by their very nature temporary and perishing; and where they proceed not from some cause in the characters and disposition of the person, who perform'd them, they infix not themselves upon him, and can neither redound to his honour, if good, nor infamy, if evil. The action in itself may be blameable. . . . But the person is not responsible for it; and as it proceeded from nothing in him, that is durable and constant, and leaves nothing of that nature behind it, 'tis impossible he can, upon its account, become the object of punishment or vengeance.[12]

Hume is surely wrong in saying that we could not praise or blame, punish or reward, a person in whose character there was nothing "permanent or durable." As he was the first to point out, we do not need any *unchanging* element in order to say that a person is the same person throughout a period of time, and our concept of merit is framed to fit our concept of personal identity. We honor people as well as nations for what they have done in the past and do not consider what has been done merely as an indication of what may be expected in the future. Moreover, it is perfectly rational to punish people for what they have done, even if there is no reason to think that they would be likely to do it again. The argument that it will be a different *me* who will be beaten tomorrow carries no weight, for "different" or not the back which will be beaten is the one about which I am concerned today. So we have no reason to invent something durable and constant underlying the actions which we punish or reward. And it is not in fact our practice to pick out for praise or blame only those actions for which something of the kind can be found. It would be possible, of course, that we should do this, punishing the cruel action of the cruel man but not that of one usually kind. But even in such a situation there would be no argument against the man who said that moral responsibility depended upon indeterminism; for a motive is not a determining cause, nor is an habitual motive. If we say that a man constantly acts out of cruelty, we no more say that his actions are determined than if we say that he acts out of cruelty on a particular occasion. There could of course be a law to the effect that no one who has been cruel for thirty years can turn to kindness after that, and this would

12 *Treatise*, bk. II, pt. III, sec. 2.

throw responsibility back from the later to the earlier acts. But it is clear that this is a special assumption in no way involved in the statement that cruelty is a "durable and constant" element in someone's character.

I have already mentioned Ayer's argument that moral responsibility cannot be defended on the basis of indeterminism and will now consider his version in detail. Ayer says that the absence of a cause will not give the moralist what he wants, because "if it is a matter of pure chance that a man should act in one way rather than another, he may be free but he can hardly be responsible." [13] To the suggestion that "my actions are the result of my own free choice," Ayer will reply with a question about how I came to make my choice:

> Either it is an accident that I choose to act as I do or it is not. If it is an accident, then it is merely a matter of chance that I did not choose otherwise; and if it is merely a matter of chance that I did not choose otherwise, it is surely irrational to hold me morally responsible for choosing as I did. But if it is not an accident that I chose to do one thing rather than another, then presumably there is some causal explanation of my choice: and in that case we are led back to determinism.[14]

The "presumably" seems to be the weak link in the argument, which assumes a straightforward opposition between causality and chance that does not in general exist. It is not at all clear that when actions or choices are called "chance" or "accidental" this has anything to do with the absence of causes, and if it has not we will not be saying that they are in the ordinary sense a matter of chance if we say that they are undetermined.

When should we say that it was a matter of chance that a man did what he did? A typical example would be the case in which a man killed someone with a bullet which glanced off some object in a totally unforeseeable way; here he could disclaim responsibility for the act. But in this instance, and that of something done "by accident," we are dealing with what is done unintentionally, and this is not the case which Ayer has in mind. We may turn, as he does, to the actions which could be said to have been "chosen" and ask how the words "chance" and "accident" apply to choices. Ayer says, "Either it is an accident that I choose to act as I do, or it is not." The notion of choosing by accident to do something is on the face of it puzzling; for usually choosing to do something is opposed to doing it by accident. What does it mean to say that the choice itself was accidental? The only application I can think of for the words "I chose by accident" is in a case such as the following. I choose a firm with which to have dealings without meaning to pick on one run by an international crook. I can now rebut the charge of *choosing a firm run by an interna-*

tional crook by saying that I chose it by accident. I cannot be held responsible for this but only for any carelessness which may have been involved. But this is because the relevant action—the one with which I am being charged—was unintentional; it is for this reason and not because my action was uncaused that I can rebut the charge. Nothing is said about my action being uncaused, and if it were, this could not be argued on my behalf; the absence of causes would not give me the same right to make the excuse.

Nor does it make any difference if we substitute "chance" for "accident." If I say that it was a matter of chance that I chose to do something, I rebut the suggestion that I chose it for this reason or for that, and this can be a plea against an accusation which has to do with my reasons. But I do not imply that there was no reason for my doing what I did, and I say nothing whatsoever about my choice being undetermined. If we use "chance" and "accident" as Ayer wants to use them, to signify the absence of causes, we shall have moved over to a totally different sense of the words, and "I chose it by chance" can no longer be used to disclaim responsibility.

"I Can"

RICHARD TAYLOR

> In philosophy it is *can* in particular that we seem so often to uncover, just when we had thought some problem settled, grinning residually up at us like the frog at the bottom of the beer mug.
>
> J. L. AUSTIN

I want to examine the idea expressed by "I can," as used in contexts implying neither special training, strength, nor opportunity. I shall not, then, be concerned with such statements as "I can speak Russian," "I can do forty push-ups," or "I can win a Rhodes Scholarship," but rather with the idea expressed in such a simple assertion as "I can move my finger." I shall begin with a consideration of four uses of "can" in contexts not involving human agency. It would be significant, I think, if this concept turned out to be essentially the same whether applied to men or to inanimate things, but it will be much more significant if, as I believe, it is essentially different.

The idea of "can" in contexts of inanimate things. Consider any statement of the form *"X can E,"* wherein X designates some inanimate object and E some state or event, such as the following:

1. A billiard ball can be both round and red (but not round and square).
2. (Lucretius thought that) atoms can swerve from their paths.
3. This can be the restaurant we ate in long ago.
4. This stone is so hot it can fry an egg.

Now these statements seem to me to express all the philosophically significant senses of "can" as applied to physical objects, and these are, respectively, three senses of *contingency*, which I shall call logical, causal,

"I Can," *The Philosophical Review,* LXIX (1960), pp. 78-89. Reprinted by permission. A revised version of a paper read at annual meetings of the American Philosophical Association, Burlington, Vermont, December 28, 1958.

and epistemic, and, in the case of fourth, the sense of a causal capacity
or, better, of *hypothetical possibility*. Our first job, then, is to make these
four meanings perfectly clear.

If we take "impossible" as a generic and undefined term, we can then
define three other ideas in terms of it in this fashion:

E is necessary $= \sim E$ is impossible.
E is possible $= \sim (E$ is impossible).
E is contingent $= \sim (\sim E$ is impossible) and $\sim (E$ is impossible).

It will be noted that the idea of the contingent, as here defined, is of that
which is neither necessary nor impossible, and it should be noted that
it is not the same as the possible; for anything which is in any sense
necessary—such as, that $2 + 2 = 4$—is in that sense also possible, but not
therefore contingent.

If we now elicit, without trying to define, three fairly familiar kinds of
impossibility, we can easily derive, by the foregoing equivalences, three
distinct senses of contingency, and these will correspond with the first
three senses of "can" illustrated above. The fourth sense, which is no
contingency at all, must be treated separately.

In the first place, then, and most obviously, a state or event is logically
impossible if the description of its occurrence is self-contradictory,[1] like
"a ball's becoming square while still spheroid." Leibniz spoke as if all
impossibilities were in principle reducible to this, and most scholars
since have supposed that it is at least the purest kind of impossibility.
But in any case something is contingent in this sense if neither the
assertion nor the denial of its occurrence involves a contradiction. We
can say of a white ball, for instance, that it can become red while still
spheroid, for these properties are logically independent.

In the second place, a state or event is, in a perfectly familiar sense,
causally impossible if there exist conditions sufficient for its non-occur-
rence or for the occurrence of something causally incompatible with it.[2]
Thus it is impossible for a man to live a happy life after he has been
beheaded, and it is impossible for gasoline-soaked rags to freeze when
brought in contact with a burning match in the open air—though no
logical impossibilities are involved in either case. Philosophers are accustomed to saying that there are no necessary connections between
events, but I believe they are only making the point that such impossibilities as these are not logical ones, which is fairly obvious. The point is
that they are, in a perfectly ordinary sense, impossibilities nonetheless; for
when a man has been decapitated, for instance, we are entitled to say not
merely that he *is* dead, but that he *has* to be dead, that he cannot be both
living and headless. The same idea is expressed by saying of any man that

---

[1] This is not meant as a definition.
[2] Neither is this meant as a definition.

if he were beheaded he would die, for this entails and is entailed by the statement that if he is beheaded he (in this sense) necessarily dies.

To say, then, that an event or state is causally contingent is equivalent to saying that neither its occurrence nor its nonoccurrence is in this sense impossible, or that existing conditions are sufficient neither for its occurrence nor for its nonoccurrence—in short, that it is uncaused. Many philosophers deny that anything in nature is contingent, in this causal sense, but this is not to the point. We are only giving a content to the idea of contingency, defined in terms of this perfectly familiar sense of impossibility, and this is the second sense of "can" illustrated above. If, for instance, it were true of a given particle that its behavior was not causally determined, then we could say that it can swerve and also that it can fail to swerve, expressing the idea that its behavior is contingent in this causal sense.

Third, something is sometimes spoken of as impossible when it is only known to be false, though this is admittedly a queer sense of "impossible." Someone might say, for example, "But that man can't be my father," and mean only that he knows he is not. I call this an epistemic sense of impossibility, and an epistemically contingent state or event is therefore one concerning which it is not known whether it occurred, or will occur, or not. This is the third sense of "can" that I illustrated and it is, in fact, exceedingly common. Thus, a man might say of a familiar-looking place that it *can* be the restaurant he ate in a year ago, at the same time realizing that it can be entirely new to him. Similarly, I might say, after tossing a normal coin but before looking to see what came up, that it can be heads and it can be tails, even though knowing that in the causal sense one or the other of these speculations is impossible. Or one might even say, of a column of figures, that its sum can be 720 or it can be 721, meaning only that he does not yet know which, even though he knows that one or the other of these is logically impossible.

Now the fourth sense of "can" which I have introduced, under the name "hypothetical possibility," is perhaps the most common of all; but, unlike the other three, it does not express any idea of contingency, but the very opposite. "Can" is, in other words, in this sense, an expression of a capacity, or of what does happen—indeed, what must happen—in case certain conditions are met. It thus conveys the idea of a causal connection between certain states or events. For example, the statement "This stone is so hot it can fry an egg" does not mean merely that it is logically contingent whether an egg fries there (though it is), nor, manifestly, that if an egg were to fry there its frying would be uncaused, nor, equally obviously, that we do not *know* what would happen to an egg if it were put there. It means that if an egg were there, it would fry—that the heat of the stone is sufficient, assuming certain other conditions to hold, for an egg's frying. And this, far from suggesting that the state of an egg in those conditions is contingent, entails the very opposite, namely, that this state is causally necessitated by those conditions, or that any other state is causally impossible.

It should be noted next, then, that the first three senses of "can," but emphatically not the fourth, can be conveyed equally by the expression "might," so understood as to mean "might and might not." Thus, I could say of a red ball that it might be white and it might be black, expressing the idea that its color is logically (though perhaps neither causally nor epistemically) contingent. Similarly, if I tossed a coin whose behavior was, let us suppose, causally undetermined, I could say that it might come heads and it might come tails, expressing the idea that the outcome is causally contingent. And finally, I could say of a familiar-looking restaurant that I might have eaten there before and I might not have, only making the point that I do not know which.

But note that if I say that a given stone is so hot that it can fry an egg, I do not mean that an egg broken there might fry and it might not. On the contrary, my whole point is that it would fry, or, under those conditions, could not *but* fry, and I mean to deny that it might not.

The "can" of human agency. Let us now turn to the idea expressed by "can" as it figures in contexts of human agency, to see whether it is essentially the same as any one or more of the above, or whether it is an idea different from any of these.

The statement "I can move my finger," as well as the statement "I can hold my finger still," are both true (though their joint truth obviously does not entail that I can do both at once). This I take to be quite certain, and if anyone doubts the truth of either, I can show him in the most direct manner possible that he should not doubt it. Hence, if there is any philosophical theory implying that one or the other of these statements must be false, then that theory is doubtful.

What, then, do I mean by "can" in such statements? Obviously, I do not mean merely that it is logically contingent whether I move my finger (although it is). If a physician were to ask me whether I can move it, he would not be inquiring whether it would be self-contradictory to suppose that I do or that I do not, for he already knows that it would not, without asking.

Nor do I mean merely that it is epistemically contingent, although perhaps it is. That is, when I say I can move my finger, the point I am making is plainly not that I do not happen to know how my finger is going to behave. If a physician were to ask me whether I can move it, he would not be asking me to guess, speculate, or hazard a prediction concerning what my finger is apt to do.

It follows, therefore, that if "can" in this context expresses an idea essentially like any I have elicited, then it expresses either the idea of causal contingency or of hypothetical possibility. The remainder of this discussion will be devoted to showing that it embodies neither of these ideas but has some different meaning altogether, and that while it entails that the event in question—a finger motion, in this case—is causally contingent (and hence, that one important version of the doctrine of "free will" is true), it is not equivalent to that doctrine.

Hypothetical possibility. Let us consider first, then, the possibility that the statement "I can move my finger" expresses simply the idea of a causal capacity, or hypothetical possibility, and is thus like the statement "This stone is so hot it can fry an egg." I must, then, like this one, express the idea that if a certain kind of event were to happen, then something else quite different—a finger motion, in this case—would follow as a result.

The statement about the stone and egg expresses, we said, the idea of a capacity or, better, the idea of a causal relationship between different events or states—an egg's being broken on a hot stone, on the one hand, and its frying, on the other—and is thus equivalent to a hypothetical in the subjunctive. If, then, the statement about my finger expresses essentially the same idea, it, too, must be equivalent to some subjunctive hypothetical expressing the idea of a causal relationship between different events or states—some as yet unnamed event or state, presumably within me, on the one hand, and a finger motion, on the other. Or, to put the same point more vividly, if I am asked by the physician whether I can move my finger and I reply that *I can,* then what I am telling him, if "can" here (as in the stone and egg case) expresses a hypothetical possibility, is that *if* there should occur within me a certain (unnamed) event or state, then the finger motion would at once follow as a causal consequence.

But that this is not what is expressed by "can" in this context, is exhibited by the fact that such hypotheticals as do undoubtedly express a genuine causal relationship between some antecedent occurrent state or event and some bodily change—such as a motion of my finger, regarded as its effect—do not convey the idea of "can" that we are seeking, together with the fact that such hypotheticals as do express this idea of "can" are mere grammatical equivalences; far from expressing any discovered or discoverable causal relationship between events or states, they express purely logical relationships between concepts, and are thereby ruled out *ab initio* as causal statements. We find, in short, that there is no hypothetical statement or set of such statements which, as in the stone and egg case, both (a) expresses the idea of a causal relationship between events or states, and (b) expresses the idea of "can" that we are after. It has been one of the most persistent errors of philosophy to suppose that, since it is not hard to find hypotheticals that express the one idea or the other, and since both kinds are hypotheticals and thus grammatically and logically similar, then some one or more of them must express both ideas at once.

Thus, it is very easy to supply subjunctive hypotheticals expressing a genuine causal relationship between some event or state within me (say), and the motion of my finger, which do not, however, convey anything like the idea of "can" that we are seeking, but which nevertheless express precisely that idea as it is involved in the stone and egg case. We can say, for instance, that if a certain muscle, well known to anatomists, were to contract, then my finger would move; but this might still be true, even if I cannot move my finger—for example, in case I cannot move the muscle in question. Again, if I happen to be subject to spasms of a certain kind, we can say that if a nerve impulse of such and such a kind were to occur, perhaps in my brain, then my finger would twitch. But this is not equivalent to saying that *I* can move my finger, for I evidently have no control over the occurrence of those impulses; nor, be it noted, does it approach any closer to saying that I can, if someone arbitrarily baptizes such an empirically discoverable nerve impulse as, say, a "volition." A physician would not conclude that I can move my finger merely upon learning that I am subject to spasms of that sort, and he might, in fact, reasonably regard it as evidence to the contrary. We at once rule out, then, such "queer" hypotheticals as these—not because they do not express the idea of a causal relationship (for manifestly they do), and not because they do not express the idea of "can" as it is embodied in the stone and egg case (for they do express that idea exactly), but because they do not express the idea of "I can."

It may be tempting at this point to suggest that "I can" expresses the idea of a causal relationship in which a very special kind of mental event fills the role of the cause—namely, a certain kind of mental thrust [3] or internal urging, well known to metaphysicians and philosophers of the mind as an act of will or of a volition. Thus, to be specific, the statement "I can move my finger" must express the idea that if there were to occur somewhere within me or within my mind a particular one of these special mental events—namely, a motion-of-this-finger volitional event—then that event would at once be followed by a motion of the finger in question, which would be its effect.

But if we refuse to be beguiled by the profundity of such a description and just look at the picture it is meant to bring forth, how absurd it becomes! Surely when I say I can move my finger and know that what I am saying is true, I am not expressing the idea of any causal connection between the behavior of my finger and some such occult internal hokus-pokus as this, the occurrence of which I can seriously doubt. Besides, even if this picture were not quite fantastic from the standpoint of ordinary experience, we can wonder whether I *can* bring about such an internal mental thrust, and in particular, whether I can perform inwardly the elaborate and complicated set of such thrusts evidently needed in order to make my finger move in a similarly elaborate and complicated way, and, if so, what "can" might mean in this case. If I can, then to what further internal events are *these* causally related? And if I cannot, how can we still say that I can move my finger after all?

[3] Cf. Gilbert Ryle, *The Concept of Mind* (London, 1949), pp. 62-69.

Not having found quite what we want in this direction, we turn more hopefully to those hypotheticals in more or less common use which do express just the idea of "can" that we are after, to see whether they might also be construed as expressing the idea of a causal relationship. But here we find that those which are usually proposed for this purpose turn out to be conventional equivalences of meaning only, rather than expressions of discovered causal connections, and that we not only have no reason whatever for supposing that they also express causal relationships between occurrent events or states but that they yield the same kind of absurdity as our previous example as soon as they are so interpreted.

It is generally supposed, for example, that such a statement as "I can move my finger" is equivalent to the hypothetical "I will move my finger if I want to." And so it is—but this is surely no expression of a causal relationship between occurrent events or states. If it were, we would have to understand it to mean that the occurrence within me of a certain state or event, of a rather special kind—namely, of a certain wanting or craving for finger motions—would set my finger in motion, which is at best a doubtful picture, such wantings as this having every semblance of fiction. If we ask someone who had just moved his finger why he had done so, and got the reply that he did so because he wanted to, we would be no wiser, recognizing that an explanation had been refused rather than given, only the fact itself being repeated that he had moved it. "I will move my finger if I want to" is essentially no different from "I'll have one more drink if I want to," uttered in a tone of defiance, or from "There are cookies in the cupboard if you want one," [4] none of which hypotheticals can in justice to common sense be construed as expressing discoverable causal connections between events or states.

For this and other reasons we must reject the other hypothetical renditions of "I can" that suggest themselves, such as "I will if I try," or "if I intend," or "if I wish," or "if I choose," or "if it suits my purpose," or "if there's any point to it," and so on. Now all these hypotheticals can, let it be noted, be regarded as equivalent in meaning to the categorical "I can." But being each of them equivalent in meaning to the same thing, they are equivalent in meaning to each other—which by itself sufficiently shows that they are not expressions of causal relations between occurrent events or states. For the events or states properly called "trying," "choosing," "wishing," "intending," "having as one's purpose," and so on—if these be regarded as events or states that might actually occur within me—are not the same, and the hypotheticals embodying these concepts, considered as referring to such occurrent states or events, cannot be equivalent in meaning; just as "There are cookies in the cupboard if you want one" has exactly the same meaning as "There are cookies in the

---

[4] Cf. J. L. Austin, *Ifs and Cans,* Annual Philosophical Lecture to the British Academy, Oxford, 1956, p. 113.

cupboard if you would like one"—but neither means anything like "There are cookies in the cupboard, if Grandmother baked this morning."

If, moreover, we ask, in the case of any such hypothetical that is seriously proposed as an expression of the relation between a cause and its effect, what might be the criterion for deciding whether it is true, we find this criterion to be the very occurrence of that event which is supposed to be regarded as the effect, rendering the relationship embodied in the hypothetical not the empirically discoverable one of a cause to its effect but a logical relationship of entailment between concepts. The fact, however, that a given event occurs can never entail that another wholly different one will occur, or has occurred, if the relation between them is that of cause to effect. The fact, for example, that an egg is broken on a certain stone cannot entail that it fries, nor vice versa, and if there were such entailment, the relation embodied in the hypothetical expressing that fact could not at the same time be regarded as one of causation. Suppose, then, that someone moves his finger and we propose as a causal explanation for this that he wanted to move it. How shall we, or the agent himself, decide whether this was in fact the cause? How do we, or how does he, know that this motion was not caused by, say, his wanting to move a different finger or even his wanting to move his toe? Has anyone had numerous occasions to observe within himself this particular want, and then come to the realization that it is in fact always soon followed by that particular motion, until he has finally come to expect the one upon finding the occurrence of the other? Plainly not. Our entire criterion for saying what he wanted (or tried, or intended, or whatnot) to do, is what he in fact did; we do not infer the former from the latter on the basis of what we have in fact found, but we regard the former as something entailed by what we now find, namely, just his moving that finger. This by itself shows that the relation expressed in the hypothetical "I will move my finger if I want to" is, if the hypothetical is true at all, a logical relationship between concepts, resting only on a conventional equivalence of meaning, and as such cannot be a causal relationship between states or events.

Causal contingency. I conclude, then, that "can," in such a context as we are considering, does not, unlike the stone and egg case, express the idea of a causal capacity or hypothetical possibility. The only thing left, therefore, if we are to suppose that it expresses a meaning similar to any it has when used with reference to physical objects, is to see if it expresses the idea of causal contingency.

In this case, the statement "I can move my finger" means that my finger might move and it might not, where "might and might not" expresses the idea that the event in question is, not merely epistemically, but causally, contingent, or that there are no conditions either causally sufficient for or causally incompatible with my finger's moving. It is easy to show, however, that this is not the meaning of "can" in this case, for it is quite possible that the statement "I can move my finger" is false, even in a situation in which "My finger might move and it might not," understood in the sense of causal contingency, is true. Suppose, for example, that I am paralyzed, so that I cannot, by hypothesis, move my finger. It is nevertheless imaginable that, despite this circumstance, my finger does move from time to time and that its motions are uncaused. No doubt this never happens but the point is that, if it were to happen, it would not warrant us in saying that I can move my finger; it just moves, in this case, without my having anything to do with it.

One other possibility remains, and that is to insist that there is an essential difference between *my* moving my finger, and my finger merely moving, and, hence, that "I can move my finger" expresses not merely the idea that any motions of my finger are causally contingent but, rather, that it is causally contingent whether *I* produce them. That there is this essential difference is beyond question, for my moving my finger is not even materially equivalent to my finger's moving, the first fact always entailing, but never being entailed by, the latter. To concede this, however, is already to abandon the possibility of understanding human agency according to the model of inanimate behavior, for in the case of the latter no such distinction ever needs to be made. The tree's waving its branches is equivalent to its branches waving, and the hot stone's frying an egg is equivalent to an egg's frying there.[5] Even in the case of robots and computing machines we can describe completely what they do merely by describing what happens (in their wires and vacuum tubes, and so forth) without any reference to their doing anything at all. Quite apart from this, however, it can be shown that while the statement "I can move my finger" entails that my moving my finger is causally contingent and, hence, that the motions of my finger are themselves causally contingent,[6] it is not equivalent to that. If this is so, then the meaning of "can," in this context, evidently does not correspond to any meaning it has in contexts involving only physical things.

The statements "I can move my finger" and "I can hold my finger still" are, we said, both true, though their joint truth does not entail that I can do both at once. If, however, existing conditions are causally sufficient for my moving my finger, then it follows that it is causally impossible for me not to move it. If, on the other hand, existing conditions are causally sufficient for my holding it still, then it is causally impossible for me to move it. Since, however, it is true both that I can move it and that I can hold it still, it follows that neither is causally impossible.

That the statement "I can move my finger" does not express just this idea, however—that is, is not equivalent to saying that I might move it and I might not, understanding this in the sense of causal contin-

---

[5] Assuming the absence of other sources of heat, etc.

[6] Given the general principle that whatever is dependent on that which is causally contingent is itself causally contingent.

gency—follows from the fact that this latter might be true in circumstances in which the former is not. That is, it might be true that it is causally contingent whether I move my finger (and not merely whether my finger moves), and yet false that I both can move it and can hold it still. Suppose, for example, that I have a roulette wheel whose behavior is really causally contingent—for instance, one whose end state is no exact function of the force with which it is spun. Suppose, further, that I resolve to move my finger if it stops on an odd number and to hold it still if it stops on an even one, and that there are conditions (the certainty of death if I fail, for instance) sufficient for my not changing my resolve. Now in this situation it is certainly true that I might move my finger and I might not, understanding "might and might not" to express causal contingency; because until the wheel stops there are no conditions sufficient for my doing the one, and none sufficient for my doing the other. Yet it is not true that I can move it, and also that I can hold it still, assuming that my resolve cannot change. I know that I might move it and that I might not, but not only do I not know whether I will move it, I do not even know—until the wheel stops and assuming that I cannot change my resolve—whether I can move it. I just have to wait and see. What I do in this situation is no longer up to me, but entirely dependent on the behavior of a wheel, over which I have no control.

"Power." I conclude, then, that "can," in the statement "I can move my finger," does not mean what it ever means when applied to physical things, although it entails what is meant by that word as it might be applied to some extraordinary physical thing, namely, one whose behavior is uncaused. What else is meant by "can," in this case, in addition to meaning that my moving my finger is causally contingent, is suggested by what was just said; namely, that whether or not I do move my finger is "up to me" or, to use a more archaic expression, is something "within my power." And this is, certainly, a philosophically baffling expression which I feel sure no one can ever analyze; yet it is something that is well understood. One can sometimes know perfectly, for example, that it is up to him or in his power to move his finger, and one can sometimes—as in the sort of example just considered—know that it is not up to him but to something else, even if it should nevertheless be contingent. We therefore understand what it is for something to be in our power, and the fact that no one can say what it is is no disconfirmation of this. This notion, however, is never embodied in the meaning of "can," as it is used with reference to physical things; for it never makes sense to say that it is up to the hot stone whether it fries an egg, or up to a tree whether it waves its branches, or that it is within the power even of a causally undetermined roulette wheel whether it picks an odd number or an even one.

III

Libertarianism

It would be hard to find a more radical or eloquent proponent of Libertarianism than Sartre. Not many would go so far as to say that man chooses his passions, or the causes of his actions. Strictly speaking, Sartre is not a defender of free will, for he conceives of the will as the mode of rational procedure with regard to ends and means, and thus opposes will to passion, which is magical procedure. In a sense, then, one must will to will—that is, one must choose to adopt rational procedure. It is consciousness rather than the will which is free for Sartre, and the freedom of consciousness consists in the power of "nihilation," which includes selective attention and the positing of "lacks" in the full and unbroken world of things. Although this selection is taken from a much more extended treatment in which this conception of consciousness is defended at length, Sartre reviews the relevant material here and the selection is self contained. We have omitted certain references to other philosophers and some illustrative material, and have appended a brief selection in which he carries through the consequences of his extreme position on human freedom to an equally extreme conception of the scope of human responsibility.

To turn from Sartre to Broad is to undergo a stylistic and methodological dislocation, but Broad's remarks are relevant even to Sartre. Broad's argument is clear enough to speak for itself, and it has been included in part because it pulls together much that lies scattered about in the other selections. Broad's primary virtue, however, is not his manner, but his point. Libertarians are very often so concerned with criticizing Determinism that they content themselves with arguments for Indeterminism; but to stop there is not to establish that actions are free in the way that Libertarians intend. Broad asks what more would be required, and instead of resting with the claim that the notion of human agency is unanalyzable, he attempts an analysis and concludes that it is impossible. Libertarians are thereby summoned to more heroic efforts than they have hitherto put forth.

From *Being and Nothingness*

JEAN-PAUL SARTRE

BEING AND DOING: FREEDOM

I. FREEDOM: THE FIRST CONDITION OF ACTION

It is strange that philosophers have been able to argue endlessly about determinism and free-will, to cite examples in favor of one or the other thesis without ever attempting first to make explicit the structures contained in the very idea of *action*. The concept of an act contains, in fact, numerous subordinate notions which we shall have to organize and arrange in a hierarchy: to act is to modify the *shape* of the world; it is to arrange means in view of an end; it is to produce an organized instrumental complex such that by a series of concatenations and connections the modification effected on one of the links causes modifications throughout the whole series and finally produces an anticipated result. But this is not what is important for us here. We should observe first that an action is on principle *intentional*. The careless smoker who has through negligence caused the explosion of a powder magazine has not *acted*. On the other hand the worker who is charged with dynamiting a quarry and who obeys the given orders has acted when he has produced the expected explosion; he knew what he was doing or, if you prefer, he intentionally realized a conscious project.

This does not mean, of course, that one must forsee all the consequences of his act. The emperor Constantine when he established himself at Byzantium, did not foresee that he would create a center of Greek culture and language, the appearance of which would ultimately provoke a schism in the Christian Church and which would contribute to weakening the Roman Empire. Yet he performed an act just in so far as he realized his project of creating a new residence for emperors in the Orient. Equating the result with the intention is here sufficient for us to be able to speak of action. But if this is the case, we establish that the action necessarily implies as its condition the recognition of a "desideratum"; that is, of an objective lack or again of a *négatité*. *The intention* of providing a rival for Rome can come to Constantine only through the apprehension of an objective lack: Rome lacks a counterweight; to this still profoundly pagan city ought to be opposed a Christian city which at the moment is *missing*. Creating Constantinople is understood as an act only if first the conception of a new city has preceded the action itself or at least if this conception serves as an organizing theme for all later steps. But this conception can not be the pure representation of the city as *possible*. It apprehends the city in its essential characteristic, which is to be a *desirable* and not yet realized possible.

This means that from the moment of the first conception of the act, consciousness has been able to withdraw itself from the full world of which it is consciousness and to leave the level of being in order frankly to approach that of non-being. Consciousness in so far as it is considered exclusively in its being, is perpetually referred from being to being and can not find in being any motive for revealing non-being. The imperial system with Rome as its capital functions positively and in a certain real way which can be easily discovered. Will someone say that the taxes are collected badly, that Rome is not secure from invasions, that it does not have the geographical location which is suitable for the capital of a Mediterranean empire which is threatened by barbarians, that its corrupt morals make the spread of the Christian religion difficult? How can anyone fail to see that all these considerations are *negative*; that is, that they aim at what is not, not at what is. To say that sixty per cent of the anticipated taxes have been collected can pass, if need be for a positive appreciation of the situation *such as it is*. To say that they are badly collected is to consider the situation across a situation which is posited as an absolute end but which precisely *is not*. To say that the corrupt morals at Rome hinder the spread of Christianity is not to consider this diffusion for what it is; that is, for a propagation at a rate which the reports of the clergy can enable us to determine. It is to posit the diffusion in itself as insufficient; that is, as suffering from a secret nothingness. But it appears as such only if it is surpassed toward a limiting-situation posited *à priori* as a value (for example, toward a certain rate of religious conversions, toward a certain mass morality). This limiting situation can not be conceived in terms of the simple consideration of the real state of things; for the most beautiful girl in the world can offer only what she has, and in the same way the most miserable situation can by itself be designated only as it *is* without any reference to an ideal nothingness.

In so far as man is immersed in the historical situation, he does not even succeed in conceiving of the failures and lacks in a political organization or determined economy; this is not, as is stupidly said, because he "is accustomed to it," but because he apprehends it in its plenitude of being and because he can not even imagine that he can exist in it otherwise. For it is necessary here to reverse common opinion and on the basis of what it is not, to acknowledge the harshness of a situation or the sufferings which it imposes, both of which are motives for conceiving of another state of affairs in which things would be better for everybody. It is on the day that we can conceive of a different state of affairs that a new light falls on our troubles and our suffering and that we *decide* that these are unbearable. A worker in 1830 is capable of revolting if his salary is lowered, for he easily conceives of a situation in which his wretched standard of living would be not as low as the one which is about to be imposed on him. But he does not represent his sufferings to himself as unbearable; he adapts himself to them not through resignation but because he lacks the education and reflection necessary for him to conceive of a social state in which these sufferings would not exist. Consequently *he does not act.* Masters of Lyon following a riot, the workers at Croix-Rousse do not know what to do with their victory; they return home bewildered, and the regular army has no trouble in overcoming them. Their misfortunes do not appear to them "habitual" but rather *natural;* they *are,* that is all, and they constitute the worker's condition. They are not detached; they are not seen in the clear light of day, and consequently they are integrated by the worker with his being. He suffers without considering his suffering and without conferring value upon it. To suffer and to *be* are one and the same for him. His suffering is the pure affective tenor of his nonpositional consciousness, but he does not *contemplate* it. Therefore this suffering can not be in itself a *motive*[1] for his acts. Quite the contrary, it is after he has formed the project of changing the situation that it will appear intolerable to him. This means that he will have had to give himself room, to withdraw in relation to it, and will have to have effected a double nihilation: on the one hand, he must posit an ideal state of affairs as a pure *present* nothingness; on the other hand, he must posit the actual situation as nothingness in relation to this state of affairs. He will have to conceive of a happiness attached to his class as a pure possible—that is, presently as a certain nothingness—and on the other hand, he will return to the present situation in order to illuminate it in the light of this nothingness and in order to nihilate it in turn by declaring: *"I am not happy."*

Two important consequences result. (1) No factual state whatever it may be (the political and economic structure of society, the psychological "state," *etc.*) is capable by itself of motivating any act whatsoever. For an

---

[1] In this and following sections Sartre makes a sharp distinction between *motif* and *mobile.* The English word "motive" expresses sufficiently adequately the French *mobile,* which refers to an inner subjective fact or attitude. For *motif* there is no true equivalent. Since it refers to an external fact or situation, I am translating it by "cause." The reader must remember, however, that this carries with it no idea of determinism. Sartre emphatically denies the existence of any cause in the usual deterministic sense. Tr.

act is a projection of the for-itself toward what is not, and what is can in no way determine by itself what is not. (2) No factual state can determine consciousness to apprehend it as a *négatité* or as a lack. Better yet no factual state can determine consciousness to define it and to circumscribe it since, as we have seen, Spinoza's statement, "Omnis determinatio est negatio," remains profoundly true. Now every action has for its express condition not only the discovery of a state of affairs as "lacking in——," i.e., as a *négatité*—but also, and before all else, the constitution of the state of things under consideration into an isolated system. There is a factual state—satisfying or not—only by means of the nihilating power of the for-itself. But this power of nihilation can not be limited to realizing a simple *withdrawal* in relation to the world. In fact in so far as consciousness is "invested" by being, in so far as it simply suffers what is, it must be included in being. It is the organized form—worker-finding-his-suffering-natural—which must be surmounted and denied in order for it to be able to form the object of a revealing contemplation. This means evidently that it is by a pure wrenching away from himself and the world that the worker can posit his suffering as unbearable suffering and consequently can *make of it the motive* for his revolutionary action. This implies for consciousness the permanent possibility of effecting a rupture with its own past, of wrenching itself away from its past so as to be able to consider it in the light of a non-being and so as to be able to confer on it the meaning which *it has* in terms of the project of a meaning which it *does not have*. Under no circumstances can the past in any way by itself produce *an act;* that is, the positing of an end which turns back upon itself so as to illuminate it. This is what Hegel caught sight of when he wrote that "the mind is the negative," although he seems not to have remembered this when he came to presenting his own theory of action and of freedom. In fact as soon as one attributes to consciousness this negative power with respect to the world and itself, as soon as the nihilation forms an integral part of the *positing* of an end, we must recognize that the indispensable and fundamental condition of all action is the freedom of the acting being.

Thus at the outset we can see what is lacking in those tedious discussions between determinists and the proponents of free will. The latter are concerned to find cases of decision for which there exists no prior cause, or deliberations concerning two opposed acts which are equally possible and possess causes (and motives) of exactly the same weight. To which the determinists may easily reply that there is no action without a *cause* and that the most insignificant gesture (raising the right hand rather than the left hand, etc.) refers to causes and motives which confer its meaning upon it. Indeed the case could not be otherwise since every action must be *intentional;* each action must, in fact, have an end, and the end in turn is referred to a cause. Such indeed is the unity of the three temporal *ekstases;* the end or temporalization of my future implies a cause (or motive); that is, it points toward my past, and the present is the upsurge of the act. To speak of an act without a cause is to speak of an act which would lack the intentional structure of every act; and the proponents of free will by searching for it on the level of the act which is in the process of being performed can only end up by rendering the act absurd. But the determinists in turn are weighting the scale by stopping their investigation with the mere designation of the cause and motive. The essential question in fact lies beyond the complex organization "cause-intention-act-end"; indeed we ought to ask how a cause (or motive) can be constituted as such.

Now we have just seen that if there is no act without a cause, this is not in the sense that we can say that there is no phenomenon without a cause. In order to be a *cause*, the *cause* must be *experienced* as such. Of course this does not mean that it is to be thematically conceived and made explicit as in the case of deliberation. But at the very least it means that the for-itself must confer on it its value as cause or motive. And, as we have seen, this constitution of the cause as such can not refer to another real and positive existence, that is, to a prior cause. For otherwise the very nature of the act as engaged intentionally in non-being would disappear. The motive is understood only by the end; that is, by the non-existent. It is therefore in itself a *négatité*. If I accept a niggardly salary it is doubtless because of fear; and fear is a motive. But it is *fear of dying from starvation*; that is, this fear has meaning only outside itself in an end ideally posited, which is the preservation of a life which I apprehend as "in danger." And this fear is understood in turn only in relation to the *value which I implicitly* give to this life; that is, it is referred to that hierarchal system of ideal objects which are values. Thus the motive makes itself understood as what it is by means of the ensemble of beings which "are not," by ideal existences, and by the future. Just as the future turns back upon the present and the past in order to elucidate them, so it is the ensemble of my projects which turns back in order to confer upon the *motive* its structure as a motive. It is only because I escape the in-itself by nihilating myself toward my possibilities that this in-itself can take on value as cause or motive. Causes and motives have meaning only inside a projected ensemble which is precisely an ensemble of non-existents. And this ensemble is ultimately myself as transcendence; it is Me in so far as I have to be myself outside of myself.

If we recall the principle which we established earlier—namely that it is the apprehension of a revolution as possible which gives to the workman's suffering its value as a motive—we must thereby conclude that it is by fleeing a situation toward our possibility of changing it that we organize this situation into complexes of causes and motives. The nihilation by which we achieve a withdrawal in relation to the situation is the same as the *ekstasis* by which we project ourselves toward a modification of this situation. The result is that it is in fact impossible to find an act without a motive but that this does not mean that we must conclude that the motive causes the act; the motive is an integral part of the act. For as the resolute project toward a change is not distinct from the act, the motive, the act, and the end are all constituted in a single upsurge. Each of these three structures claims the two others as its meaning. But the organized totality of the three is no longer explained by any particular structure, and its upsurge as the pure temporalizing nihilation of the in-itself is one with freedom. It is the act which decides its ends and its motives, and the act is the expression of freedom. . . .

In our attempt to reach the heart of freedom we may be helped by the few observations which we have made on the subject in the course of this work and which we must summarize here. In the first chapter we established the fact that if negation comes into the world through human reality, the latter must be a being who can realize a nihilating rupture with the world and with himself; and we established that the permanent possibility of this rupture is the same as freedom. But on the other hand, we stated that this permanent possibility of nihilating what I am in the form of "having-been" implies for man a particular type of existence. We were able then to determine by means of analyses like that of bad faith that human reality is its own nothingness. For the for-itself, to be is to nihilate the in-itself which it is. Under these conditions freedom can be nothing other than this nihilation. It is through this that the for-itself escapes its being as its essence; it is through this that the for-itself is always something other than what can be *said* of it. For in the final analysis the For-itself is the one which escapes this very denomination, the one which is already beyond the name which is given to it, beyond the property which is recognized in it. To say that the for-itself has to be what it is, to say that it is what it is not while not being what it is, to say that in it existence precedes and conditions essence or inversely according to Hegel, that for it "Wesen ist was gewesen ist"—all this is to say one and the same thing: to be aware that man is free. Indeed by the sole fact that I am conscious of the causes which inspire my action, these causes are already transcendent objects for my consciousness; they are outside. In vain shall I seek to catch hold of them; I escape them by my very existence. I am condemned to exist forever beyond my essence, beyond the causes and motives of my act. I am condemned to be free. This means that no limits to my freedom can be found except freedom itself or, if you prefer, that we are not free to cease being free. To the extent that the for-itself wishes to hide its own nothingness from itself and to incorporate the in-itself as its true mode of being, it is trying also to hide its freedom from itself.

The ultimate meaning of determinism is to establish within us an unbroken continuity of existence in itself. The motive conceived as a psychic fact—i.e., as a full and given reality—is, in the deterministic view, articulated without any break with the decision and the act, both of which are equally conceived as psychic givens. The in-itself has got hold of all these "data"; the motive provokes the act as the physical cause its effect; everything is real, everything is full. Thus the refusal of freedom can be conceived only as an attempt to apprehend oneself as being-in-itself; it amounts to the same thing. Human reality may be defined as a being such that in its being its freedom is at stake because human reality perpetually tries to refuse to recognize its freedom. Psychologically in each one of us this amounts to trying to take the causes and motives as *things*. We try to confer permanence upon them. We attempt to hide from ourselves that their nature and their weight depend each moment on the meaning which I give to them; we take them for constants. This amounts to considering the meaning which I gave to them just now or yesterday—which is irremediable because it is *past*—and extrapolating from it a character fixed still in the present. I attempt to persuade myself that the cause *is* as it was. Thus it would pass whole and untouched from my past consciousness to my present consciousness. It would inhabit my consciousness. This amounts to trying to give an essence to the for-itself. In the same way people will posit ends as transcendences, which is not an error. But instead of seeing that the transcendences there posited are maintained in their being by my own transcendence, people will assume that I encounter them upon my surging up in the world; they come from God, from nature, from "my" nature, from society. These ends ready made and pre-human will therefore define the meaning of my act even before I conceive it, just as causes as pure psychic givens will produce it without my even being aware of them.

Cause, act, and end constitute a *continuum*, a *plenum*. These abortive attempts to stifle freedom under the weight of being (they collapse with the sudden upsurge of anguish before freedom) show sufficiently that freedom in its foundation coincides with the nothingness which is at the heart of man. Human-reality is free because it *is not enough*. It is free because it is perpetually wrenched away from itself and because it has been separated by a nothingness from what it is and from what it will be. It is free, finally, because its present being is itself a nothingness in the form of the "reflection-reflecting." Man is free because he is not himself but presence to himself. The being which is what it is can not be free. Freedom is precisely the nothingness which is *made-to-be* at the heart of man and which forces human-reality *to make itself* instead of *to be*. As we have seen, for human reality, to be is to *choose oneself*; nothing comes to it either from the outside or from within which it can receive or accept. Without any help whatsoever, it is entirely abandoned to the intolerable necessity of making itself be—down to the slightest detail. Thus freedom is not a being; it is *the being* of man—i.e., his nothingness of being. If we start by conceiving of man as a plenum, it is absurd to try to find in him afterwards moments or psychic regions in which he would be free. As well look for emptiness in a container which one has filled beforehand up to the brim! Man can not be sometimes slave and sometimes free; he is wholly and forever free or he is not free at all.

These observations can lead us, if we know how to use them, to new discoveries. They will enable us first to bring to light the relations between freedom and what we call the "will." There is a fairly common tendency to seek to identify free acts with voluntary acts and to restrict the deterministic explanation to the world of the passions. In short the point of view of Descartes. The Cartesian will is free, but there are "passions of the soul." Again Descartes will attempt a physiological interpretation of these passions. Later there will be an attempt to instate a purely psychological determinism. Intellectualistic analyses such as Proust, for example, attempts with respect to jealousy or snobbery can serve as illustrations for this concept of the passional "mechanism." In this case it would be necessary to conceive of man as simultaneously free and determined, and the essential problem would be that of the relations between this unconditioned freedom and the determined processes of the psychic life: how will it master the passions, how will it utilize them for its own benefit? A wisdom which comes from ancient times—the wisdom of the Stoics—will teach us to come to terms with these passions so as to master them; in short it will counsel us how to conduct ourselves with regard to affectivity as man does with respect to nature in general when he obeys it in order better to control it. Human reality therefore appears as a free power besieged by an ensemble of determined processes. One will distinguish wholly free acts, determined processes over which the free will has power, and processes which on principle escape the human-will.

It is clear that we shall not be able to accept such a conception. But let us try better to understand the reasons for our refusal. There is one objection which is obvious and which we shall not waste time in developing; this is that such a trenchant duality is inconceivable at the heart of the psychic unity. How in fact could we conceive of a being which could be one and which nevertheless on the one hand would be constituted as a series of facts determined by one another—hence existents in exteriority—and which on the other hand would be constituted as a spontaneity determining itself to be and revealing only itself? A priori this spontaneity would be capable of no action on a determinism already *constituted*. On what could it act? On the object itself (the present psychic fact)? But how could it modify an in-itself which by definition is and can be only what it is? On the actual law of the process? This is self-contradictory. On the antecedents of the process? But it amounts to the same thing whether we act on the present psychic fact in order to modify it in itself or act upon it in order to modify its consequences. And in each case we encounter the same impossibility which we pointed out earlier. Moreover, what instrument would this spontaneity have at its disposal? If the hand can clasp, it is because it can be clasped. Spontaneity, since by definition it is *beyond reach* can not in turn *reach*; it can produce only itself. And if it could dispose of a special instrument, it would then be necessary to conceive of this as of an intermediary nature between free will and determined passions—which is not admissible. For different reasons the passions could get no hold upon the will. Indeed it is impossible for a determined process to act upon a spontaneity, exactly as it is impossible for objects to act upon consciousness. Thus any synthesis of two types of existents is impossible; they are not homogeneous; they will remain each one in its incommunicable solitude. The only bond which a nihilating spontaneity could maintain with mechanical processes would be the fact that it *produces itself by an internal negation directed toward these existents.* But then the spontaneity will exist precisely only in so far as it denies concerning itself that it is these passions. Henceforth the ensemble of the determined πάθος will of necessity be apprehended by spontaneity as a pure transcendent; that is, as what is necessarily *outside,* as what *is not it.*[2] This internal negation would therefore have for its effect only the dissolution of the πάθος in the world, and the πάθος would exist as some sort of object in the midst of the world for a free spontaneity which would be simultaneously will and consciousness. This discussion shows that two solutions and only two are possible: either man is wholly determined (which is inadmissible, especially because a determined consciousness—i.e., a consciousness externally motivated—becomes itself pure exteriority and ceases to be consciousness) or else man is wholly free.

But these observations are still not our primary concern. They have only a negative bearing. The study of the will should, on the contrary, enable us to advance further in our understanding of freedom. And this is why the fact which strikes us first is that if the will is to be autonomous, then it is impossible for us to consider it as a *given* psychic fact; that is, in-itself. It can not belong to the category defined by the psychologist as "states of consciousness." Here as everywhere else we assert that the state of consciousness is a pure idol of a positive psychology. If the will is to be freedom, then it is of necessity negativity and the power of nihilation. But then we no longer can see why autonomy should be preserved for the will. In fact it is hard to conceive of those holes of nihilation which would be the volitions and which would surge up in the otherwise dense and full web of the passions and of the πάθος in general. If the will is nihilation, then the ensemble of the psychic must likewise be nihilation. Moreover—and we shall soon return to this point—where do we get the idea that the "fact" of passion or that pure, simple desire is not nihilating? Is not passion first a project and an enterprise? Does it not exactly posit a state of affairs as intolerable? And is it not thereby forced to effect a withdrawal in relation to this state of affairs and to nihilate it by isolating it and by considering it in the light of an end—i.e., of a non-being? And does not passion have its own ends which are recognized precisely at the

[2] I.e., is not spontaneity. Tr.

same moment at which it posits them as non-existent? And if nihilation is precisely the being of freedom, how can we refuse autonomy to the passions in order to grant it to the will?

But this is not all: the will, far from being the unique or at least the privileged manifestation of freedom, actually—like every event of the for-itself—must presuppose the foundation of an original freedom in order to be able to constitute itself as will. The will in fact is posited as a reflective decision in relation to certain ends. But it does not create these ends. It is rather a mode of being in relation to them: it decrees that the pursuit of these ends will be reflective and deliberative. Passion can posit the same ends. For example, if I am threatened, I can run away at top speed because of my fear of dying. This passional fact nevertheless posits implicitly as a supreme end the value of life. Another person in the same situation will, on the contrary, understand that he must remain at his post even if resistance at first appears more dangerous than flight; he "will stand firm." But his goal, although better understood and explicitly posited, remains the same as in the case of the emotional reaction. It is simply that the methods of attaining it are more clearly conceived; certain of them are rejected as dubious or inefficacious, others are more solidly organized. The difference here depends on the choice of means and on the degree of reflection and of making explicit, not on the end. Yet the one who flees is said to be "passionate," and we reserve the term "voluntary" for the man who resists. Therefore the question is of a difference of subjective attitude in relation to a transcendent end. But if we wish to avoid the error which we denounced earlier and not consider these transcendent ends as pre-human and as an a priori limit to our transcendence, then we are indeed compelled to recognize that they are the temporalizing projection of our freedom. Human reality can not receive its ends, as we have seen, either from outside or from a so-called inner "nature." It chooses them and by this very choice confers upon them a transcendent existence as the external limit of its projects. From this point of view—and if it is understood that the existence of the *Dasein* precedes and commands its essence—human reality in and through its very upsurge decides to define its own being by its ends. It is therefore the positing of my ultimate ends which characterizes my being and which is identical with the sudden thrust of the freedom which is mine. And this thrust is an existence; it has nothing to do with an essence or with a property of a being which would be engendered conjointly with an idea.

Thus since freedom is identical with my existence, it is the foundation of ends which I shall attempt to attain either by the will or by passionate efforts. Therefore it can not be limited to voluntary acts. Volitions, on the contrary, like passions are certain subjective attitudes by which we attempt to attain the ends posited by original freedom. By original freedom, of course, we should not understand a freedom which would be *prior* to the voluntary or passionate act but rather a foundation which is strictly contemporary with the will or the passion and which these *manifest,* each in its own way. Neither should we oppose freedom to the will or to passion as the "profound self" of Bergson is opposed to the superficial self; the for-itself is wholly selfness and can not have a "profound self," unless by this we mean certain transcendent structures of the psyche. Freedom is nothing but the *existence* of our will or of our passions in so far as this existence is the nihilation of facticity; that is, the existence of a being which is its being in the mode of having to be it. We shall return to this point. In any case let us remember that the will is determined within the compass of motives and ends already posited by the for-itself in a transcendent projection of itself toward its possibles. If this were not so, how could we understand deliberation, which is an evaluation of means in relation to already existing ends?

If these ends are already posited, then what remains to be decided at each moment is the way in which I shall conduct myself with respect to them; in other words, the attitude which I shall assume. Shall I act by volition or by passion? Who can decide except me? In fact, if we admit that circumstances decide for me (for example, I can act by volition when faced with a minor danger but if the peril increases, I shall fall into passion), we thereby suppress all freedom. It would indeed be absurd to declare that the will is autonomous when it appears but that external circumstances strictly determine the moment of its appearance. But, on the other hand, how can it be maintained that a will which does not yet exist can suddenly decide to shatter the chain of the passions and suddenly stand forth on the fragments of these chains? Such a conception would lead us to consider the will as a *power* which sometimes would manifest itself to consciousness and at other times would remain hidden, but which would in any case possess the permanence and the existence "in-itself" of a property. This is precisely what is inadmissible. It is, however, certain that common opinion conceives of the moral life as a struggle between a will-thing and passion-substances. There is here a sort of psychological Manichaeism which is absolutely insupportable.

Actually it is not enough to will; it is necessary to will to will. Take, for example, a given situation: I can react to it emotionally. We have shown elsewhere that emotion is not a physiological tempest,[3] it is a reply adapted to the situation; it is a type of conduct, the meaning and form of which are the object of an intention of consciousness which aims at attaining a particular end by particular means. In fear, fainting and cataplexie[4] aim at suppressing the danger by suppressing the consciousness of the danger. There is an *intention* of losing consciousness in order

[3] *Esquisse d'une théorie phenomenologique des emotions,* Hermann, 1939. In English, *The Emotions: Outline of a Theory.* Tr. by Bernard Frechtman. Philosophical Library, 1948.
[4] A word invented by Preyer to refer to sudden inhibiting numbness produced by any shock. Tr.

to do away with the formidable world in which consciousness is engaged and which comes into being through consciousness. Therefore we have to do with magical behavior provoking the symbolic satisfactions of our desires and revealing by the same stroke a magical stratum of the world. In contrast to this conduct voluntary and rational conduct will consider the situation scientifically, will reject the magical, and will apply itself to realizing determined series and instrumental complexes which will enable us to resolve the problems. It will organize a system of means by taking its stand on instrumental determinism. Suddenly it will reveal a technical world; that is, a world in which each instrumental-complex refers to another larger complex and so on. But what will make me decide to choose the magical aspect or the technical aspect of the world? It can not be the world itself, for this in order to be manifested waits to be discovered. Therefore it is necessary that the for-itself in its project must choose being the one by whom the world is revealed as magical or rational; that is, the for-itself must as a free project of itself give to itself magical or rational existence. It is responsible for either one, for the for-itself can be only if it has chosen itself. Therefore the for-itself appears as the free foundation of its emotions as of its volitions. My fear *is* free and manifests my freedom; I have put all my freedom into my fear, and I have chosen myself as fearful in this or that circumstance. Under other circumstances I shall exist as deliberate and courageous, and I shall have put all my freedom into my courage. In relation to freedom there is no privileged psychic phenomenon. All my "modes of being" manifest freedom equally since they are all ways of being my own nothingness.

This fact will be even more apparent in the description of what we called the "causes and motives" of action. We have outlined that description in the preceding pages; at present it will be well to return to it and take it up again in more precise terms. Did we not say indeed that passion is the *motive* of the act—or again that the passional act is that which has passion for its motive? And does not the will appear as the decision which follows deliberation concerning causes and motives? What then is a cause? What is a motive?

Generally by cause we mean the *reason* for the act; that is, the ensemble of rational considerations which justify it. If the government decides on a conversion of Government bonds, it will give the causes for its act: the lessening of the national debt, the rehabilitation of the Treasury. . . . What motivates the conversion of the bonds is the state of the national debt. Nevertheless this objective appreciation can be made only in the light of a presupposed end and within the limits of a project of the for-itself toward this end. . . . We shall therefore use the term cause for the objective apprehension of a determined situation as this situation is revealed in the light of a certain end as being able to serve as the means for attaining this end.

The motive, on the contrary, is generally considered as a subjective fact. It is the ensemble of the desires, emotions, and passions which urge me to accomplish a certain act. The historian looks for motives and takes them into account only as a last resort when the causes are not sufficient to explain the act under consideration. . . . The explanation must then be sought in the psychic state—even in the "mental" state—of the historical agent. It follows naturally that the event becomes wholly contingent since another individual with other passions and other desires would have acted differently. In contrast to the historian the psychologist will by preference look for motives; usually he supposes, in fact, that they are "contained in" the state of consciousness which has provoked the action. The ideal rational act would therefore be the one for which the motives would be practically nil and which would be uniquely inspired by an objective appreciation of the situation. The irrational or passionate act will be characterized by the reverse proportion.

It remains for us to explain the relation between causes and motives in the everyday case in which they exist side by side. For example, I can join the Socialist party because I judge that this party serves the interests of justice and of humanity or because I believe that it will become the principal historical force in the years which will follow my joining: these are causes. And at the same time I can have motives: a feeling of pity or charity for certain classes of the oppressed, a feeling of shame at being on the "good side of the barricade," as Gide says, or again an inferiority complex, a desire to shock my relatives, etc. What can be meant by the statement that I have joined the Socialist party for these causes *and* these motives? Evidently we are dealing with two radically distinct layers of meaning. How are we to compare them? How are we to determine the part played by each of them in the decision under consideration? This difficulty, which certainly is the greatest of those raised by the current distinction between causes and motives, has never been resolved; few people indeed have so much as caught a glimpse of it. Actually under a different name it amounts to positing the existence of a conflict between the will and the passions. But if the classic theory is discovered to be incapable of assigning to cause and motive their proper influence in the simple instance when they join together to produce a single decision, it will be wholly impossible[5] for it to explain or even to conceive of a conflict between causes and motives, a conflict in which each group would urge its individual decision. Therefore we must start over again from the beginning.

To be sure, the cause is objective; it is the state of contemporary things as it is revealed to a consciousness. It is *objective* that the Roman plebs and aristocracy were corrupted by the time of Constantine or that the Catholic Church is ready to favor a monarch who at the time of Clovis will help it triumph over Arianism. Nevertheless this state of affairs can

---

[5] Sartre says "wholly possible" (*tout à fait possible*) which I feel sure is a misprint. Tr.

be revealed only to a for-itself since in general the for-itself is the being by which "there is" a world. Better yet, it can be revealed only to a for-itself which chooses itself in this or that particular way—that is, to a for-itself which has made its own individuality. The for-itself must of necessity have projected itself in this or that way in order to discover the instrumental implications of instrumental-things. Objectively the knife is an instrument made of a blade and a handle. I can grasp it objectively as an instrument to slice with, to cut with. But lacking a hammer, I can just as well grasp the knife as an instrument to hammer with. I can make use of its handle to pound in a nail, and this apprehension is no less *objective*. . . . But this potentiality can be revealed only if the situation is surpassed toward a state of things which does not yet exist—in short, towards a nothingness. In a word the world gives counsel only if one questions it, and one can question it only for a well determined end.

Therefore the cause, far from determining the action, appears only in and through the project of an action. . . .

Thus cause and motive are correlative as the non-thetic self-consciousness is the ontological correlate of the thetic consciousness of the object. Just as the consciousness of something is self-consciousness, so the motive is nothing other than the apprehension of the cause in so far as this apprehension is self-consciousness. But it follows obviously that the cause, the motive, and the end are the three indissoluble terms of the thrust of a free and living consciousness which projects itself toward its possibilities and makes itself defined by these possibilities.

How does it happen then that the motive appears to the psychologist as the affective content of a fact of consciousness as this content determines another fact of consciousness or a decision? It is because the motive which is nothing other than a non-thetic self-consciousness, slips into the past with this same consciousness and along with it ceases to be living. As soon as a consciousness is made-past, it is what I have to be in the form of the "was." Consequently when I turn back toward my consciousness of yesterday, it preserves its intentional significance and its meaning as subjectivity, but, as we have seen, it is fixed; it is outside like a thing, since the past is in-itself. The motive becomes then that *of which* there is consciousness. It can appear to me in the form of "empirical knowledge"; as we saw earlier, the dead past haunts the present in the aspect of a *practical knowing*. It can also happen that I turn back toward it so as to make it explicit and formulate it while guiding myself by the knowledge which it is for me in the present. In this case it is an object of consciousness; it is this very consciousness *of which I am conscious*. It appears therefore—like my memories in general—simultaneously as *mine* and as transcendent. Ordinarily we are surrounded by these motives which we "no longer enter," for we not only have to decide concretely to accomplish this or that act but also to accomplish actions which we decided upon the day before or to pursue enterprises in which we are engaged. In a general way consciousness at whatever moment it is grasped is apprehended as engaged and this very apprehension implies a practical knowing of the motives of the engagement or even a thematic and positional explanation of these causes. It is obvious that the apprehension of the motive refers at once to the cause, its correlate, since the motive, even when made-past and fixed in in-itself, at least maintains as its meaning the fact that it has been a consciousness of a cause; i.e., the discovery of an objective structure of the world. But as the motive is *in-itself* and as the cause is objective, they are presented as a dyad without ontological distinction; we have seen, indeed, that our past is lost in the midst of the world. That is why we put them on the same level and why we are able to speak of the causes *and* of the motives of an action as if they could enter into conflict or both concur in determined proportion in a decision.

Yet if the motive is transcendent, if it is only the irremediable being which we have to be in the mode of the "was," if like all our past it is separated from us by a breadth of nothingness, then it can act only if it is *recovered;* in itself it is without force. It is therefore by the very thrust of the engaged consciousness that a value and a weight will be conferred on motives and on prior causes. What they have been does not depend on consciousness, but consciousness has the duty of maintaining them in their existence in the past. I have willed this or that: here is what remains irremediable and which even constitutes my essence, since my essence is what I have been. But the meaning held for me by this desire, this fear, these objective considerations of the world when presently I project myself toward my futures—this must be decided by me alone. I determine them precisely and only by the very act by which I project myself toward my ends. The recovery of former motives—or the rejection or new appreciation of them—is not distinct from the project by which I assign new ends to myself and by which in the light of these ends I apprehend myself as discovering a supporting cause in the world. Past motives, past causes, present motives and causes, future ends, all are organized in an indissoluble unity by the very upsurge of a freedom which is beyond causes, motives and ends.

The result is that a voluntary deliberation is always a deception. How can I evaluate causes and motives on which I myself confer their value before all deliberation and by the very choice which I make of myself? The illusion here stems from the fact that we endeavor to take causes and motives for entirely transcendent things which I balance in my hands like weights and which possess a weight as a permanent property. Yet on the other hand we try to view them as contents of consciousness, and this is self-contradictory. Actually causes and motives have only the weight which my project—i.e., the free production of the end and of the known act to be realized—confers upon them. When I deliberate, the chips are down.[6] And if I am brought to the point of deliberating, this is simply because it is a part of my original project to realize motives by means of *deliberation* rather than by some other form of discovery (by passion, for example, or simply by action, which reveals to me the organized ensemble of causes and of ends as my language informs me of my thought). There is therefore a choice of deliberation as a procedure which will make known to me what I project and consequently what I am. And *the choice* of deliberation is organized with the ensemble motives-causes and end by free spontaneity. When the will intervenes, the decision is taken, and it has no other value than that of making the announcement. . . .

III. FREEDOM AND RESPONSIBILITY

Although the considerations which are about to follow are of interest primarily to the ethicist, it may nevertheless be worthwhile after these descriptions and arguments to return to the freedom of the for-itself and to try to understand what the fact of this freedom represents for human destiny.

The essential consequence of our earlier remarks is that man being condemned to be free carries the weight of the whole world on his shoulders; he is responsible for the world and for himself as a way of being. We are taking the word "responsibility" in its ordinary sense as "consciousness (of) being the incontestable author of an event or of an object." In this sense the responsibility of the for-itself is overwhelming since he[7] is the one by whom it happens that *there* is a world; since he is also the one who makes himself be, then whatever may be the situation in which he finds himself, the for-itself must wholly assume this situation with its peculiar coefficient of adversity, even though it be insupportable. He must assume the situation with the proud consciousness of being the author of it, for the very worst disadvantages or the worst threats which can endanger my person have meaning only in and through my project; and it is on the ground of the engagement which I am that they appear. It is therefore senseless to think of complaining since nothing foreign has decided what we feel, what we live, or what we are.

Furthermore this absolute responsibility is not resignation; it is simply the logical requirement of the consequences of our freedom. What happens to me happens through me, and I can neither affect myself with it nor revolt against it nor resign myself to it. Moreover everything which happens to me is *mine*. By this we must understand first of all that I am

[6] *Les jeux sont faits.* Sartre has written a novel by this title. Tr.

[7] I am shifting to the personal pronoun here since Sartre is describing the for-itself in concrete personal terms rather than as a metaphysical entity. Strictly speaking, of course, this is his position throughout, and the French *"il"* is indifferently "he" or "it." Tr.

always equal to what happens to me *qua* man, for what happens to a man through other men and through himself can be only human. The most terrible situations of war, the worst tortures do not create a non-human state of things; there is no non-human situation. It is only through fear, flight, and recourse to magical types of conduct that I shall decide on the non-human, but this decision is human, and I shall carry the entire responsibility for it. But in addition the situation is mine because it is the image of my free choice of myself, and everything which it presents to me is *mine* in that this represents me and symbolizes me. Is it not I who decide the coefficient of adversity in things and even their unpredictability by deciding myself?

Thus there are no *accidents* in a life; a community event which suddenly burst forth and involves me in it does not come from the outside. If I am mobilized in a war, this war is *my* war; it is in my image and I deserve it. I deserve it first because I could always get out of it by suicide or by desertion; these ultimate possibles are those which must always be present for us when there is a question of envisaging a situation. For lack of getting out of it, I have *chosen* it. This can be due to inertia, to cowardice in the face of public opinion, or because I prefer certain other values to the value of the refusal to join in the war (the good opinion of my relatives, the honor of my family, etc.). Anyway you look at it, it is a matter of a choice. This choice will be repeated later on again and again without a break until the end of the war. Therefore we must agree with the statement by J. Romains, "In war there are no innocent victims."[8] If therefore I have preferred war to death or to dishonor, everything takes place as if I bore the entire responsibility for this war. Of course others have declared it, and one might be tempted perhaps to consider me as a simple accomplice. But this notion of complicity has only a juridical sense, and it does not hold here. For it depended on me that for me and by me this war should not exist, and I have decided that it does exist. There was no compulsion here, for the compulsion could have got no hold on a freedom. I did not have any excuse; for as we have said repeatedly in this book, the peculiar character of human-reality is that it is without excuse. Therefore it remains for me only to lay claim to this war.

But in addition the war is *mine* because by the sole fact that it arises in a situation which I cause to be and that I can discover it there only by engaging myself for or against it, I can no longer distinguish at present the choice which I make of myself from the choice which I make of the war. To live this war is to choose myself through it and to choose it through my choice of myself. There can be no question of considering it as "four years of vacation" or as a "reprieve," as a "recess," the essential part of my responsibilities being elsewhere in my married, family, or pro-

---

[8] J. Romains: *Les hommes de bonne volonté;* "Prélude à Verdun."

fessional life. In this war which I have chosen I choose myself from day to day, and I make it mine by making myself. If it is going to be four empty years, then it is I who bear the responsibility for this.

Finally, as we pointed out earlier, each person is an absolute choice of self from the standpoint of a world of knowledges and of techniques which this choice both assumes and illumines; each person is an absolute upsurge at an absolute date and is perfectly unthinkable at another date. It is therefore a waste of time to ask what I should have been if this war had not broken out, for I have chosen myself as one of the possible meanings of the epoch which imperceptibly let to war. I am not distinct from this same epoch; I could not be transported to another epoch without contradiction. Thus *I am* this war which restricts and limits and makes comprehensible the period which preceded it. In this sense we may define more precisely the responsibility of the for-itself if to the earlier quoted statement, "There are no innocent victims," we add the words, "We have the war we deserve." Thus, totally free, undistinguishable from the period for which I have chosen to be the meaning, as profoundly responsible for the war as if I had myself declared it, unable to live without integrating it in *my* situation, engaging myself in it wholly and stamping it with my seal, I must be without remorse or regrets as I am without excuse; for from the instant of my upsurge into being, I carry the weight of the world by myself alone without anything or any person being able to lighten it.

Yet this responsibility is of a very particular type. Someone will say, "I did not ask to be born." This is a naive way of throwing greater emphasis on our facticity. I am responsible for everything, in fact, except for my very responsibility, for I am not the foundation of my being. Therefore everything takes place as if I were compelled to be responsible. I am *abandoned* in the world, not in the sense that I might remain abandoned and passive in a hostile universe like a board floating on the water, but rather in the sense that I find myself suddenly alone and without help, engaged in a world for which I bear the whole responsibility without being able, whatever I do, to tear myself away from this responsibility for an instant. For I am responsible for my very desire of fleeing responsibilities. To make myself passive in the world, to refuse to act upon things and upon Others is still to choose myself, and suicide is one mode among others of being-in-the-world. Yet I find an absolute responsibility for the fact that my facticity (here the fact of my birth) is directly inapprehensible and even inconceivable, for this fact of my birth never appears as a brute fact but always across a projective reconstruction of my for-itself. I am ashamed of being born or I am astonished at it or I rejoice over it, or in attempting to get rid of my life I affirm that I live and I assume this life as bad. Thus in a certain sense I *choose* being born. This choice itself is integrally affected with facticity since I am not able not to choose, but this facticity in turn will appear only in so far as I surpass it toward my ends. Thus facticity is everywhere but inapprehensible; I never encounter anything except my responsibility. That is why I can not ask, "*Why* was I born?" or curse the day of my birth or declare that I did not ask to be born, for these various attitudes toward my birth—i.e., toward the *fact* that I realize a presence in the world—are absolutely nothing else but ways of assuming this birth in full responsibility and of making it *mine*. Here again I encounter only myself and my projects so that finally my abandonment—i.e., my facticity—consists simply in the fact that I am condemned to be wholly responsible for myself. I am the being which *is* in such a way that in its being its being is in question. And this "is" of my being *is* as present and inapprehensible.

Under these conditions since every event in the world can be revealed to me only as an *opportunity* (an opportunity made use of, lacked, neglected, etc.), or better yet since everything which happens to us can be considered as a *chance* (i.e., can appear to us only as a way of realizing this being which is in question in our being) and since others as transcendences-transcended are themselves only *opportunities* and *chances,* the responsibility of the for-itself extends to the entire world as a peopled-world. It is precisely thus that the for-itself apprehends itself in anguish; that is, as a being which is neither the foundation of its own being nor of the Other's being nor of the in-itselfs which form the world, but a being which is compelled to decide the meaning of being—within it and everywhere outside of it. The one who realizes in anguish his condition as *being* thrown into a responsibility which extends to his very abandonment has no longer either remorse or regret or excuse; he is no longer anything but a freedom which perfectly reveals itself and whose being resides in this very revelation. But as we pointed out at the beginning of this work, most of the time we flee anguish in bad faith.

Determinism, Indeterminism, and Libertarianism

C. D. BROAD

THE IMPLICATIONS OF OBLIGABILITY

We often make retrospective judgments about the past actions of ourselves or other people which take the form: "You ought not to have done the action X, which you in fact did; you ought instead to have done the action Y, which in fact you did not." If I make such a judgment about a person, and he wants to refute it, he can take two different lines of argument. (1) He may say: "I could have done Y instead of X, but you are mistaken in thinking that Y was the action that I ought to have done. In point of fact, X, the action that I did, was the one that I ought to have done. If I had done Y, I should have done what I ought not to have done." (2) He may say: "I could not help doing X," or he may say: "Though I need not have done X, I could not possibly have done Y."

If the accused person makes an answer of the first kind, he is admitting that the alternatives "ought" and "ought not" apply to the actions X and Y, but he is objecting to my applying "ought" to Y and "ought not" to X. He is saying that "ought" applies to X, and "ought not" to Y. It is as if two people, who agree that X and Y are each either black or white, should differ because one holds that X is black and Y white whilst the other holds that X is white and Y black. If the accused person makes an answer of the second kind, he is denying the applicability of the alternatives "ought" and "ought not." If he says: "I could not help doing X," he assumes that his critic will admit neither "ought" nor "ought not" has any application to an action which the agent could not help doing. If he says: "Though I need not have done X, yet I could not possibly have done Y," he assumes that his critic will admit that neither "ought" nor "ought not" has any application to an action which the agent could not have done. It is as if one person should say that X is black and Y is white, and the other should answer that at least one of them is unextended and therefore incapable of being either black or white.

OBLIGABILITY ENTAILS SUBSTITUTABILITY

Now we are concerned here only with the second kind of answer. The essential point to notice is that it is universally admitted to be a *relevant* answer. We all admit that there is some sense or other of "could" in which "ought" and "ought not" entail "could." We will now try to get clear about the connexion between these two notions.

Judgments of obligation about past actions may be divided into two classes, viz. (1) judgments about actions which were actually done, and (2) judgments about conceivable actions which were not done. Each divides into two sub-classes, and so we get the following fourfold division. (1·1) "You did X, and X was the action that you ought to have done." (1·2) "You did X, and X was an action that you ought not to have done." (2·1) "You did not do X, and X was the action that you ought to have done." And (2·2) "You did not do X, and X was an action that you ought not to have done." Now both judgments of the first class entail that you could have helped doing the action which you in fact did. If the action that you did can be said to be one that you ought to have done, or if it can be said to be one that you ought not to have done, it must be one that you *need not* have done. And, since you actually did it, it is obviously one that you *could have* done. Both judgments of the second class entail that you could have done an action which you did not in fact do. If a conceivable action which you did not do can be said to be one which you ought to have done, or if it can be said to be one that you ought not to have done, it must be one that you *could have* done. And, since you actually failed to do it, it is obviously one that you *need not* have done.

It is worth while to notice that the common phrases: "You ought to have done so and so" and "You ought not to have done so and so" are generally equivalent to our judgments (2·1) and (1·2) respectively. The former is generally used to mean: "You did not do so and so, and that was an action which you ought to have done." The latter is generally used to mean: "You did so and so, and that was an action which you ought not to have done." But we often need to express what is expressed by our judgments (1·1) and (2·2). We often want to say that a person did what he ought on a certain occasion, and we often want to say that a person avoided doing something which he ought not to have done on a certain occasion. For this is exactly the state of affairs which exists when a person has in fact done an unpleasant duty in face of a strong temptation to shirk it by lying.

Now the importance of this connexion between "ought" and "ought not," on the one hand, and "could," on the other, is very great. People constantly make judgments of obligation of the four kinds which we have distinguished, and such judgments have constantly been made throughout the whole course of human history. Every single one of these judgments has been false unless there have been cases in which actions which *were* done could have been left undone and actions which *were not* done could have been done. And these judgments would all have been false in principle, and not merely in detail. They would have been false, not in the sense that they asserted "ought" where they should have asserted "ought not," or *vice versa*. They would be false in the sense that nothing in the world has ever had that determinable characteristic of which "ought to be done" and "ought not to be done" are the determinate specifications. They would be false in the sense in which all judgments which predicated redness, blueness, etc., of any object would be false in a world which contained no objects except minds and noises.

It will be convenient to call an action "obligable" if and only if it is an action of which "ought to be done" or "ought not to be done" can be predicated. It will be convenient to call an action "substitutable" if, either it was done but could have been left undone, or it was left undone but could have been done. We may then sum up the situation by saying that an action is obligable if and only if it is, in a certain sense, substitutable; that, unless all judgments of obligations are false in principle, there are obligable actions; and therefore, unless all judgments of obligation are false in principle, there are actions which are, in this sense, substitutable.

VARIOUS SENSES OF "SUBSTITUTABLE"

This is one aspect of the case. The other aspect is the following. There are several senses of "could" in which nearly everyone would admit that some actions which were done could have been left undone, and some actions which were left undone could have been done. There are thus several senses of "substitutable" in which it would commonly be admitted that some actions are substitutable. But, although an action which was *not* substitutable in these senses would *not* be obligable, it seems doubtful whether an action which was substitutable *only* in these senses *would be* obligable. It seems doubtful whether an action would be obligable unless it were substitutable in some further sense.

At this stage two difficulties arise. (i) It is extremely difficult to grasp and to express clearly this further sense of "substitutable," i.e. this further sense of "could" in which an action that was done could have been left undone or an action which was not done could have been done. Many people would say that they can attach no meaning to "substitutable" except those meanings in which it is insufficient to make an action obligable. (ii) Even if this other meaning of "substitutable" can be grasped and clearly expressed, many people would say that no action is substitutable in this sense. They would claim to see that no action which has been done could have been left undone, and that no action which was not done could have been done, in that sense of "could" which is required if an action is to be obligable.

Now anyone who holds these views is in a very awkward position. On the one hand, it is not easy to believe that every judgement of obligation is false, in the sense in which every judgment ascribing color to an object would be false in a world containing only minds and noises. On the other hand, it is highly depressing to have to admit that there is a sense of "could" which you can neither grasp nor clearly express. And it is equally unsatisfactory to have to believe that some actions *are* substitutable in a sense in which it seems to you self-evident that no action *could be* substitutable.

There are two problems to be tackled at this point. (i) To try to discover and state the sense of "substitutable" in which being substitutable is the necessary and sufficient condition of being obligable. And (ii), if we can do this, to consider whether any action could be substitutable in this sense.

VOLUNTARY SUBSTITUTABILITY

Let us begin by considering an action which has actually been performed. In some cases we should say that the agent "could not have helped" performing it. We should certainly say this if we had reason to believe that the very same act would have been performed by the agent in these circumstances even though he had willed that it should not take place. It is obvious that there are actions which are "inevitable," in this sense, since there are actions which take place although the agent is trying his hardest to prevent them. Compare, e.g. the case of a conspirator taken with an uncontrollable fit of sneezing.

Next consider a conceivable action which was not in fact performed. In some cases we should say that the agent "could not possibly" have performed it. We should certainly say this if the act would not have taken place in these circumstances no matter how strongly the agent had willed it. It is obvious that there are conceivable acts which are "impossible" in this sense, since there are cases where such an act fails to take place although the agent is trying his hardest to bring it about. Compare, e.g. the case of a man who is bound and gagged, and tries vainly to give warning to a friend.

We will call acts of these two kinds "not voluntarily substitutable." It is plain that an act which is not voluntarily substitutable is not obligable. No one would say that the conspirator ought not to have sneezed, or that the bound and gagged man ought to have warned his friend. At most we may be able to say that they ought or ought not to have done certain things in the past which are relevant to their present situation. Perhaps the conspirator ought to have sprayed his nose with cocaine before hiding behind the presumably dusty arras, and perhaps the victim ought not to have let himself be lured into the house in which he was gagged and bound. But these are previous questions.

We see then that to be voluntarily substitutable is a *necessary* condition for an action to be obligable. But is it a *sufficient* condition? Suppose I performed the action A on a certain occasion. Suppose that I should not have done A then if I had willed with a certain degree of force and persistence not to do it. Since I did A, it is certain that I *did not* will with this degree of force and persistence to avoid doing it. Now suppose that at the time I *could not* have willed with this degree of force and persistence to avoid doing A. Should we be prepared to say that I ought not to have done A?

Now take another case. Suppose that on a certain occasion I failed to do a certain conceivable action B. Suppose that I should have done B if I had willed with a certain degree of force and persistence to do it. Since I did not do B, it is certain that I *did not* will with this degree of force and persistence to do it. Now suppose that at the time I *could not* have willed with this degree of force and persistence to do B. Should we be prepared to say that I ought to have done B? It seems to me almost certain that, under the supposed conditions, we should not be prepared to say either that I ought not to have done A or that I ought to have done B.

Consider, e.g. the case of a man who gradually becomes addicted to some drug like morphine, and eventually becomes a slave to it. At the early stages we should probably hold that he could have willed with enough force and persistence to insure that the temptation would be resisted. At the latest stages we should probably hold that he could not have done so. Now at every stage, from the earliest to the latest, the hypothetical proposition would be true: "If he had willed with a certain degree of force and persistence to avoid taking morphine, he would have avoided taking it." Yet we should say at the earlier stages that he ought to have resisted, whilst, at the final stages, we should be inclined to say that "ought" and "ought not" have ceased to apply.

PRIMARY AND SECONDARY SUBSTITUTABILITY

An action which was in fact done, but would not have been done if there had been a strong and persistent enough desire in the agent not to do it, will be called "primarily avoidable." Suppose, in addition, that there could have been in the agent at the time a desire of sufficient strength and persistence to prevent the action being done. Then the action might be called "secondarily avoidable." If this latter condition is not fulfilled, we shall say that the action was "primarily avoidable, but secondarily inevitable." Similarly, an action which was not in fact done, but would have been done if there had been in the agent a strong and persistent enough desire to do it, will be called "primarily possible."

Suppose, in addition, that there could have been in the agent at the time a desire of sufficient strength and persistence to insure the action being done. Then the action may be called "secondarily possible." If this latter condition is not fulfilled, we shall say that the action is "primarily possible, but secondarily impossible." An action will be called "primarily substitutable" if it is either primarily avoidable or primarily possible. It will be secondarily substitutable if it is either secondarily avoidable or secondarily possible. In order that an action may be obligable it is not enough that it should be primarily substitutable, it must be at least secondarily substitutable.

We are thus led on from the notion of voluntarily substitutable *actions* to that of substitutable *volitions*. Suppose that, on a certain occasion and in a certain situation, a certain agent willed a certain alternative with a certain degree of force and persistence. We may say that the volition was substitutable if the same agent, on the same occasion and in the same circumstances, could instead have willed a different alternative or could have willed the same alternative with a different degree of force and persistence. Now there is one sense of "could" in which it might plausibly be suggested that many volitions are substitutable. It seems very likely that there are many occasions on which I *should* have willed otherwise than I did, *if* on previous occasions I had willed otherwise than I did. So it seems likely that many volitions have been voluntarily substitutable.

It is necessary to be careful at this point, or we may be inadvertently granting more than we are really prepared to admit. Obviously it is often true that, if I had willed otherwise than I did on certain earlier occasions, I should never have got into the position in which I afterwards made a certain decision. If, e.g. Julius Caesar had decided earlier in his career not to accept the command in Gaul, he would never have been in the situation in which he decided to cross the Rubicon. This, however, does not make his decision to cross the Rubicon substitutable. For a volition is substitutable only if a different volition could have occurred in the agent in the *same* situation. Again, it is often true that, if I had willed otherwise than I did on certain earlier occasions, my state of knowledge and belief would have been different on certain later occasions from what it in fact was. In that case I should have thought, on these later occasions, of certain alternatives which I did not and could not think of in my actual state of knowledge and belief. Suppose, e.g. that a lawyer has to decide what to do when a friend has met with an accident. If this man had decided years before to study medicine instead of law, it is quite likely that he would now think of, and perhaps choose, an alternative which his lack of medical knowledge prevents him from contemplating. This, however, does not make the lawyer's volition in the actual situation substitutable. For, although the external part of the total situation might have been the same whether he had previously decided to study medicine or to study law, the internal part of the total situation would have been different if he had decided to study medicine, instead of deciding, as he did, to study law. He would have become an agent with different cognitive powers and dispositions from those which he in fact has. No one would think of saying that the lawyer ought to have done a certain action, which he did not and could not contemplate, merely because he would have contemplated it and would have decided to do it if he had decided years before to become a doctor instead of becoming a lawyer.

Having cleared these irrelevances away, we can now come to the real point. A man's present conative-emotional dispositions, and what we may call his "power of intense and persistent willing," are in part dependent on his earlier volitions. If a person has repeatedly chosen the easier of the alternatives open to him, it becomes increasingly difficult for him to choose and to persist in pursuing the harder of two alternatives. If he has formed a habit of turning his attention away from certain kinds of fact, it will become increasingly difficult for him to attend fairly to alternatives which involve facts of these kinds. This is one aspect of the case. Another, and equally important, aspect is the following. If a man reflects on his own past decisions, he may see that he has a tendency to ignore or to dwell upon certain kinds of fact, and that this had led him to make unfair or unwise decisions on many occasions. He may decide that, in future, he will make a special effort to give due, and not more than due, weight to those considerations which he has a tendency to ignore or to dwell upon. And this decision may make a difference to his future decisions. On the other hand, he may see that certain alternatives have a specially strong attraction for him, and he may find that, if he pays more than a fleeting attention to them, he will be rushed into choosing them, and will afterwards regret it. He may decide that, in future, he will think as little as possible about such alternatives. And this decision may make a profound difference to his future decisions.

We can now state the position in general terms. Suppose that, if the agent had willed differently on earlier occasions, his conative-emotional dispositions and his knowledge of his own nature would have been so modified that he would now have willed differently in the actual external situation and in his actual state of knowledge and belief about the alternatives open to him. Then we can say that his actual volition in the present situation was "voluntarily avoidable," and that a volition of a different kind or of a different degree of force and persistence was "voluntarily possible." An action which took place was secondarily avoidable if the following two conditions are fulfilled. (i) That this action would not have been done if the agent had willed with a certain degree of force and persistence to avoid it. (ii) That, if he had willed differently in the past, his conative-emotional dispositions and his knowledge of his own nature would have been such, at the time when he did the action, that he would have willed to avoid it with enough force and persistence to prevent him doing it. In a precisely similar way we could define the statement that a certain conceivable action which was not done, was secondarily possible. And we can thus define the statement that an action is secondarily substitutable.

Can we say that an action is obligable if it is secondarily substitutable, in the sense just defined, though it is not obligable if it is only primarily substitutable? It seems to me that the same difficulty which we noticed before reappears here. Suppose that the agent could not have willed otherwise than he did in the remoter past. It is surely irrelevant to say that, *if* he had done so, his conative dispositions *would* have been different at a later stage from what they in fact were then, and that he *would* have willed otherwise than he then did. One might, of course, try to deal with this situation by referring back to still earlier volitions. One might talk of actions which are not only primarily, or only secondarily, but are tertiarily substitutable. But it is quite clear that this is useless. If neither primary nor secondary substitutability, in the sense defined, suffice to make an action obligable, no higher order of substitutability, in this sense, will suffice. The further moves are of exactly the same nature as the second move. And so, if the second move does not get us out of the difficulty, none of the further moves will do so.

CATEGORICAL SUBSTITUTABILITY

The kind of substitutability which we have so far considered may be called "conditional substitutability." For at every stage we have defined "could" to mean "would have been, if certain conditions had been fulfilled which were not." Now I have concluded that merely conditional substitutability, of however high an order, is not a sufficient condition for obligability. If an action is to be obligable, it must be *categorically* substitutable. We must be able to say of an action, which was done, that it could have been avoided, in some sense of "could" which is not definable in terms of "would have, if." And we must be able to say of a conceivable action, which was not done, that it could have been done, in some sense of "could" which is not definable in terms of "would have, if." Unless there are some actions of which such things can truly be said, there are no actions which are obligable. We must therefore consider whether any clear meaning can be attached to the phrase "categorically substitutable," i.e. whether "could" has any clear meaning except "would have, if." And, if we can find such a meaning, we must inquire whether any actions are categorically substitutable.

VARIOUS SENSES OF "OBLIGABLE"

Before tackling these questions I must point out that the words "ought" and "ought not" are used in several different senses. In some of these senses obligability does not entail categorical substitutability.

(i) There is a sense of "ought" in which we apply it even to inanimate objects. It would be quite proper to say: "A car ought to be able to get from London to Cambridge in less than three hours," or: "A fountain-pen ought not to be constantly making blots." We mean by this simply that a car which did take more than three hours would be a poor specimen of car, or would be in a bad state of repair. And similar remarks apply to the statement about the fountain-pen. We are comparing the behaviour of a certain car or fountain-pen with the average standard of achievement of cars or fountain-pens. We are not suggesting that *this* car or *this* pen, in its present state of repair, unconditionally could go faster or avoid making blots. Sometimes when we make such judgments we are comparing an individual's achievements, not with those of the *average* member, but with those of an *ideally perfect* member, of a certain class to which it belongs. We will call "ought," in this sense, "the comparative ought." And we can then distinguish "the average-comparative ought" and "the ideal-comparative ought."

(ii) Plainly "ought" and "ought not" can be, and often are, used in this sense of human actions. But, in the case of human actions, there is a further development. Since a human being has the power of cognition, in general, and of reflexive cognition, in particular, he can have an idea of an average or an ideal man. He can compare his own achievements with those of the average, or the ideal, man, as conceived by him. And he will have a more or less strong and persistent desire to approximate to the ideal and not to fall below the average. Now it is part of the notion of an ideal man that he is a being who would have a high ideal of human nature and would desire strongly and persistently to approximate to his ideal. Obviously it is no part of the notion of an ideal horse or an ideal car that it is a being which would have a high ideal of horses or cars and a strong and persistent desire to live up to this. When we say that a man ought not to cheat at cards we often mean to assert two things. (*a*) That the average decent man does not do this, and that anyone who does falls in this respect below the average. And (*b*) that a man who does this either has a very low ideal of human nature or a very weak and unstable desire to approximate to the ideal which he has. So that, in this further respect, he falls below the average.

Now neither of these judgments implies that a particular person, who cheated on a particular occasion, categorically could have avoided cheating then; or that he categorically could have had a higher ideal of human nature; or that he categorically could have willed more strongly and persistently to live up to the ideal which he had. For an action to be obligable, in this sense, it is plain enough that it should be secondarily substitutable, in the sense already defined.

THE CATEGORICAL OUGHT

Some philosophers of great eminence, e.g. Spinoza, have held that the sense of "ought" which I have just discussed is the only sense of it. Plainly it is a very important sense, and it is one in which "ought" and "ought not" can be applied only to the actions of intelligent beings with power of reflexive cognition, emotion, and conation. I think that a clear-headed Determinist should hold either that this is the only sense; or that, if there is another sense, in which obligability entails *categorical* substitutability, it has no application.

Most people, however, would say that, although we often do use "ought" and "ought not" in this sense, we quite often use them in another sense, and that in this other sense they entail categorical substitutability. I am inclined to think that this is true. When I judge that I ought not to have done something which I in fact did, I do not as a rule seem to be judging merely that a person with higher ideals, or with a stronger and more persistent desire to live up to his ideals, would not have done what I did. Even when this is part of what I mean, there seems to be something more implied in my judgment, viz. that I *could* have had higher ideals or *could* have willed more strongly and persistently to live up to my ideals, where "could" does not mean just "would have, if." Let us call this sense of "ought" the "categorical ought." It seems to me then that we must distinguish between an action being obligable in the comparative sense and being obligable in the categorical sense; and that, if any action were categorically obligable, it would have to be categorically substitutable.

ANALYSIS OF CATEGORICAL SUBSTITUTABILITY

We can now proceed to discuss the notion of categorical substitutability. It seems to me to involve a negative and a positive condition. I think that the negative condition can be clearly formulated, and that there is no insuperable difficulty in admitting that it may sometimes be fulfilled. The ultimate difficulty is to give any intelligible account of the positive condition. I will now explain and illustrate these statements.

Suppose that, on a certain occasion, I willed a certain alternative with a certain degree of force and persistence, and that, in consequence of this volition, I did a certain voluntary action which I should not have done unless I had willed this alternative with this degree of intensity and persistence. To say that I categorically could have avoided doing this action implies at least that the following negative condition is fulfilled. It implies that the process of my willing this alternative with this degree of force and persistence was not completely determined by the nomic, the occurrent, the dispositional, and the background conditions which existed immediately before and during this process of willing. In order to see exactly what this means it will be best to contrast it with a case in which we believe that a process is completely determined by such conditions.

Suppose that two billiard-balls are moving on a table, that they collide at a certain moment, and that they go on moving in modified directions with modified velocities in consequence of the impact. Let us take as universal premisses the general laws of motion and of elastic impact. We will call these "nomic premisses." Let us take as singular premisses the following propositions. (i) That each ball was moving in such and such a direction and with such and such a velocity at the moment of impact. We will call this an "occurrent premiss." (ii) That the masses and co-efficients of elasticity of the balls were such and such. We will call this a "dispositional premiss." (iii) That the table was smooth and level before, at, and after the moment of impact. We will call this a "background premiss." Lastly, let us take the proposition that the balls are moving, directly after the impact, in such and such directions with such and such velocities. Then this last proposition is a *logical consequence* of the conjunction of the nomic, the occurrent, the dispositional, and the background premisses. That is to say, the combination of these premisses with the denial of the last proposition would be *logically inconsistent*. It is so in exactly the sense in which the combination of the premisses of a valid syllogism with the denial of its conclusion would be so.

We can now work towards a definition of the statement that a certain event e was completely determined in respect of a certain characteristic. When we have defined this statement it will be easy to define the statement that a certain event was not completely determined in respect of a certain characteristic. I will begin with a concrete example, and will then generalize the result into a definition.

Suppose that a certain flash happened at a certain place and date. This will be a manifestation of a certain determinable characteristic, viz. color, in a certain perfectly determinate form. It may, e.g. be a red flash of a certain perfectly determinate shade, intensity, and saturation. We may call shade, intensity, and saturation the three "dimensions" of color, and we shall therefore symbolize the determinable characteristic color by a three-suffix symbol C_{123}. When we want to symbolize a certain perfectly determinate value of this we shall use the symbol C_{123}^{abc}. This means that the shade has the determinate value a, that the intensity has the determinate value b, and that the saturation has the determinate value c. Each *index* indicates the determinate value which the dimension indicated by the corresponding *suffix* has in the given instance.

Now the statement that this flash was completely determined in respect of color has the following meaning. It means that there is a set of true nomic, occurrent, dispositional, and background propositions which together entail the proposition that a manifestation of color, of the precise shade, intensity, and saturation which this flash manifested, would happen at the place and time at which this flash happened. To say that this flash was *not* completely determined in respect of color means that there is *no* set of true nomic, occurrent, dispositional, and background propositions which together entail the propositions that a manifestation of color, of the precise shade, intensity, and saturation which this flash manifested, would happen at the place and time at which this flash happened.

There are two remarks to be made at this point. (i) It seems to me that the second statement is perfectly *intelligible,* even if no such statement be ever true. (ii) It is a purely *ontological* statement, and not in any way a statement about the limitations of our knowledge. Either there is such a set of true propositions, or there is not. There may be such a set, even if no one knows that there is; and there may be no such set, even if everyone believes that there is.

We can now give a general definition. The statement that a certain event e was completely determined in respect of a certain determinable characteristic C_{123} is equivalent to the conjunction of the following two propositions. (i) The event e was a manifestation of C_{123} in a certain perfectly determinate form C_{123}^{abc} at a certain place and date. (ii) There is a set of true nomic, occurrent, dispositional, and background propositions which together entail that a manifestation of C_{123} in the form C_{123}^{abc} would happen at the place and date at which e happened. The statement that e was *not* completely determined in respect of C_{123} is equivalent to the conjoint assertion of (i) and denial of (ii).

The next point to notice is that an event might be partly determined and partly undetermined in respect of a certain characteristic. As before, I will begin with a concrete example. Our flash might be completely determined in respect of shade and saturation, but not in respect of intensity. This would be equivalent to the conjunction of the following two statements. (i) That there is a set of true propositions, of the kind already mentioned, which together entail that a flash, of precisely the shade and saturation which this flash had, would happen at the place and date at which this flash happened. (ii) There is no such set of true propositions which together entail that a flash, of precisely the intensity which this flash had, would happen at the time and place at which this flash happened. We thus get the notion of "orders of indetermination" in respect of a given characteristic. If an event is undetermined in respect of one and only one dimension of a certain determinable characteristic, we say that it has "indetermination of the first order" in respect of this characteristic. If it is undetermined in respect of two and only two dimensions of a certain determinable characteristic, we say that it has "indetermination of the second order" in respect of this characteristic. And so on.

It is obvious that there is another possibility to be considered, which I will call "range of indetermination in respect of a given dimension of a given characteristic." Suppose that our flash is undetermined in respect of the intensity of its color. There may be a set of true propositions, of the kind mentioned, which together entail that a flash, whose intensity falls within certain limits, would happen at the time and place at which this flash happened. This range of indetermination may be wide or narrow. Complete determination in respect of a given dimension of a given characteristic is the limiting case where the range of indetermination shuts up to zero about the actual value of this dimension for this event. Thus the "extent of indetermination" of an event with respect to a given characteristic depends in general upon two factors, viz. (i) its order of indetermination with respect to the dimensions of this characteristic, and (ii) its range of indetermination with respect to those dimensions for which it is not completely determined.

We can now define the statement that a certain event *e* was completely determined. It means that *e* has zero range of indetermination for every dimension of every determinable characteristic of which it is a manifestation. The statement that a certain event *e* was *not* completely determined can now be defined. It means that *e* had a finite range of indetermination for at least one dimension of at least one of the characteristics of which it was a manifestation.

And now at last we can define "determinism" and "indeterminism." Determinism is the doctrine that *every* event is completely determined, in the sense just defined. Indeterminism is the doctrine that some, and it may be all, events are not completely determined, in the sense defined. Both doctrines are, *prima facie*, intelligible, when defined as I have defined them.

There is one other point to be noticed. An event might be completely determined, and yet it might have a "causal ancestor" which was not completely determined. If *Y* is the total cause of *Z* and *X* is the total cause of *Y*, I call both *Y* and *X* "causal ancestors" of *Z*. Similarly, if *W* were the total cause of *X*, I should call *Y*, *X*, and *W* "causal ancestors" of *Z*. And so on. If at any stage in such a series there is a term, e.g. *W*, which contains a cause-factor that is not completely determined, the series will stop there, just as the series of human ancestors stops with Adam. Such a term may be called the "causal progenitor" of such a series. If determinism be true, every event has causal ancestors, and therefore there are no causal progenitors. If ineterminism be true, there are causal progenitors in the history of the world.

We can now state the negative condition which must be fulfilled if an action is to be categorically substitutable. Suppose that, at a certain time, an agent deliberated between two alternatives, *A* and *B*, and that he actually did *A* and not *B*. Suppose that the following conditions are fulfilled.

(i) The doing of A by this agent at this moment was completely determined. (ii) The total cause of A being done contained as cause-factors a desire of a certain strength and persistence for A and a desire of a certain strength and persistence for B. (iii) These two desires were not completely determined in respect of strength and persistence. (iv) The range of indetermination was wide enough to include in it, as possible values, so strong and persistent a desire for B or so weak and fleeting a desire for A as would have determined the doing of B instead of the doing of A. Conditions (iii) and (iv) are the negative conditions which must be fulfilled if B is to be categorically substitutable for A. They amount to the following statement. It is consistent with (*a*) the laws of nature, including those of psychology, (*b*) the facts about the agent's dispositions and the dispositions of any other agent in the world at the moment of acting, (*c*) the facts about what was happening within and without the agent at that moment, and (*d*) the facts about the general background conditions at that moment, that the strength and persistence of the desires mentioned in (ii) should have any value that falls within the range mentioned in (iv).

Before we go further there is one point to be mentioned. Strictly speaking, what I have just stated are the negative conditions for *primary* categorical substitutability. For I have supposed the incomplete determination to occur at the *first* stage backwards, viz. in one of the cause-factors in the total cause of the action A. It would be quite easy to define, in a similar way, the negative conditions for secondary, or tertiary, or any other order of categorical substitutability. All that is needed is that, at *some* stage in the causal ancestry of A, there shall be a total cause which contains as factors desires of the agent answering to the conditions which I have stated. That is to say, all that is necessary is that A shall have a causal ancestor which is a causal progenitor, containing as a factor an incompletely determined desire of the agent's.

We come now to the final question. Supposing that this negative condition were fulfilled, would this *suffice* to make an action categorically obligable? It seems to me plain that it would not. Unless some further and positive condition were fulfilled, all that one could say would be the following: "The desire to do A happened to be present in me with such strength and persistence, as compared with the desire to do B, that I did A and avoided B. The desire to do B might have happened to be present in me with such strength and persistence, as compared with the desire to do A, that I should have done B and avoided A." Now, if this is all, the fact and I did A and not B is, in the strictest sense, an *accident,* lucky or unlucky as the case may be. It may be welcomed or it may be deplored, but neither I nor anything else in the universe can properly be praised or blamed for it. It begins to look as if the categorical ought may be inapplicable, though for different reasons, both on the hypothesis that voluntary actions have causal progenitors and on the hypothesis that none of their causal ancestors are causal progenitors.

THE POSITIVE CONDITION

Let us now try to discover the positive conditions of categorical obligability. I think that we should naturally tend to answer the sort of objection which I have just raised in the following way. We should say: "I deliberately identified myself with my desire to do *A*, or I deliberately threw my weight on the side of that desire. I might instead have made no particular effort in one direction or the other; or I might have identified myself with, and thrown my weight on the side of, my desire to do *B*. So my desire to do *A* did not just happen to be present with the requisite strength and persistence, as compared with my desire to do *B*. It had this degree of strength and persistence because, and only because, I *reinforced* it by a deliberate effort, which I need not have made at all and which I could have made in favour of my desire to do *B*." Another way of expressing the same thing would be this: "I forced myself to do *A*; but I need not have done so, and, if I had not done so, I should have done *B*." Or again: "I might have forced myself to do *B*; but I did not, and so I did *A*."

It is quite plain that these phrases express a genuine positive experience with which we are all perfectly familiar. They are all, of course, metaphorical. It will be noticed that they all attempt to describe the generic fact by metaphors drawn from specific instances of it, e.g. deliberately pressing down one scale of a balance, deliberately joining one side in a tug-of-war, deliberately thrusting a body in a certain direction against obstacles, and so on. In this respect they may be compared with attempts to describe the generic facts about time and change by metaphors drawn from specific instances, such as flowing streams, moving spots of light, and so on. The only use of such metaphors is to direct attention to the sort of fact which one wants one's hearers to contemplate. They give no help towards analysing or comprehending this fact. A metaphor helps us to understand a fact only when it brings out an analogy with a fact of a *different* kind, which we already understand. When a generic fact can be described only by metaphors drawn from specific instances of itself it is a sign that the fact is unique and peculiar, like the fact of temporal succession and the change of events from futurity, through presentness, to pastness.

Granted that there is this unique and peculiar factor of deliberate effort or reinforcement, how far does the recognition of it help us in our present problem? So far as I can see, it merely takes the problem one step further back. My doing of *A* is completely determined by a total cause which contains as factors my desire to do *A* and my desire to do *B*, each of which has a certain determinate strength and persistence. The preponderance of my desire to do *A* over my desire to do *B*, in respect of strength and persistence, is completely determined by a total cause which contains as a factor my putting forth a certain amount of effort to reinforce my desire for A. This *effort-factor* is not completely determined. It is logically consistent with all the nomic, occurrent, dispositional, and background facts that no effort should have been made, or that it should have been directed towards reinforcing the desire for B instead of the desire for A, or that it should have been put forth more or less strongly than it actually was in favor of the desire for A. Surely then we can say no more than that it just happened to occur with a certain degree of intensity in favor of the desire for A.

I think that the safest course at this stage for those who maintain that some actions are categorically obligable would be the following. They should admit quite frankly what I have just stated, and should then say: "However paradoxical it may seem, we do regard ourselves and other people as morally responsible for accidents of this unique kind, and we do not regard them as morally responsible, in the categorical sense, for anything but such accidents and those consequences of them which would have been different if the accidents had happened differently. Only such accidents, and their causal descendants in the way of volition and action, are categorically obligable." If anyone should take up this position, I should not know how to refute him, though I should be strongly inclined to think him mistaken.

This is not, however, the position which persons who hold that some actions are categorically obligable generally do take at this point. I do not find that they ever state quite clearly what they think they believe, and I suspect that is because, if it were clearly stated, it would be seen to be impossible. I shall therefore try to state clearly what I think such people want to believe, and shall try to show that it is impossible. I suspect that they would quarrel with my statement that, on their view, the fact that one puts forth such and such an effort in support of a certain desire is, in the strictest sense, an accident. They would like to say that the putting forth of a certain amount of effort in a certain direction at a certain time *is* completely determined, but is determined in a unique and peculiar way. It is literally determined *by the agent or self*, considered as a substance or continuant, and not by a total cause which contains as factors *events* in and *dispositions of* the agent. If this could be maintained, our puttings-forth of effort would be completely determined, but their causes would neither be events nor contain events as cause-factors. Certain series of events would then originate from causal progenitors which are continuants and not events. Since the first event in such a series would be completely determined, it would not be an accident. And, since the total cause of such an event would not be an event and would not contain an event as a cause-factor, the two alternatives "completely determined" and "partially undetermined" would both be inapplicable to it. For these alternatives apply only to events.

I am fairly sure that this is the kind of proposition which people who profess to believe in free will want to believe. I have, of course, stated it with a regrettable crudity, of which they would be incapable. Now it seems to me clear that such a view is impossible. The putting-forth of an effort of a certain intensity, in a certain direction, at a certain moment, for a certain duration, is quite clearly an event or process, however unique and peculiar it may be in other respects. It is therefore subject to any conditions which self-evidently apply to every event, as such. Now it is surely quite evident that, if the beginning of a certain process at a certain time is determined at all, its total cause *must* contain as an essential factor another event or process which *enters into* the moment from which the determined event or process *issues.* I see no *prima facie* objection to there being events that are not completely determined. But, in so far as an event *is* determined, an essential factor in its total cause must be other *events.* How could an event possibly be determined to happen at a certain date if its total cause contained no factor to which the notion of date has any application? And how can the notion of date have any application to anything that is not an event?

Of course I am well aware that we constantly use phrases, describing causal transactions, in which a continuant is named as the cause and no event in that continuant is mentioned. Thus we say: "The stone broke the window," "The cat killed the mouse," and so on. But it is quite evident that all such phrases are elliptical. The first, e.g. expresses what would be more fully expressed by the sentence: "The coming in contact of the moving stone with the window at a certain moment caused a process of disintegration to begin in the window at that moment." Thus the fact that we use and understand such phrases casts no doubt on the general principle which I have just enunciated.

Let us call the kind of causation which I have just described and rejected "non-occurrent causation of events." We will call the ordinary kind of causation, which I had in mind when I defined "determinism" and "indeterminism," "occurrent causation."

Now I think we can plausibly suggest what may have made some people think they believe that puttings-forth of effort are events which are determined by non-occurrent causation. It is quite usual to say that a man's putting-forth of effort in a certain direction on a certain occasion was determined by "Reason" or "Principle" or "Conscience" or "The Moral Law." Now these impressive names and phrases certainly do not denote events or even substances. If they denote anything, they stand for propositions or systems of propositions, or for those peculiar universals or systems of universals which Plato called "Ideas." If it were literally true that puttings-forth of effort are determined by such entities, we should have causation of events in time by timeless causes. But, of course, statements like "Smith's putting-forth of effort in a certain direction on a certain occasion was determined by the Moral Law" cannot be taken literally. The Moral Law, as such, has no causal efficacy. What is meant is

that Smith's *belief* that a certain alternative would be in accordance with
the Moral Law, and his *desire* to do what is right, were cause-factors in
the total cause which determined his putting-forth of effort on the side of
that alternative. Now this belief was an event, which happened when he
began to reflect on the alternatives and to consider them in the light of
the moral principles which he accepts and regards as relevant. And this
desire was an event, which happened when his conative emotional moral
dispositions were stirred by the process of reflecting on the alternatives.
Thus the use of phrases about action being "determined by the Moral
Law" may have made some people think they believe that some events
are determined by non-occurrent causation. But our analysis of the meaning of such phrases shows that the facts which they express give no logical
support to this belief.

LIBERTARIANISM

We are now in a position to define what I will call "libertarianism."
This doctrine may be summed up in two propositions. (i) Some (and it
may be all) voluntary actions have a causal ancestor which contains as a
cause-factor the putting-forth of an effort which is not completely determined in direction and intensity by occurrent causation. (ii) In such
cases the direction and the intensity of the effort are completely determined by non-occurrent causation, in which the self or agent, taken as a
substance or continuant, is the non-occurrent total cause. Thus, libertarianism, as defined by me, entails indeterminism, as defined by me; but
the converse does not hold.

If I am right, libertarianism is self-evidently impossible, whilst indeterminism is *prima facie* possible. Hence, if categorical obligability entails
libertarianism, it is certain that no action can be categorically obligable.
But if categorical obligability entails only indeterminism, it is *prima facie*
possible that some actions are categorically obligable. Unfortunately, it
seems almost certain that categorical obligability entails more than indeterminism, and it seems very likely that it entails libertarianism. It is
therefore highly probable that the notion of categorical obligability is a
delusive notion, which neither has nor can have any application.

IV

The Voluntary

As we have indicated earlier, the customary point of departure in moral life and legal practice for the philosophical problem of free will is the concept of voluntary action, and to embark on that problem presupposes some confidence in our understanding of voluntariness.

But long ago Plato counseled against such confidence, remarking that "we have never achieved any clear demarcation between these two types of wrongs, the voluntary and the involuntary, which are recognized as distinct by every legislator who ever existed in any society and regarded as distinct by all law. . . ." [1] Aristotle took up the task of clarification indicated by Plato, and his results are to be found in two extended examinations of the voluntary. We have included a selection from the *Eudemian Ethics*, once believed to be the work of a disciple, but now widely accepted as Aristotle's own and probably written somewhat earlier than his more widely read *Nicomachean Ethics*, because it is centered around the question of psychological compulsion, a question much discussed in his time and that is important in ours as well. In the *Nicomachean Ethics*, Aristotle does not dwell so much on this question of compulsion as he does on the problem of culpable ignorance. It should be noted that a more exact but less idiomatic translation of the word given here as "choice" would be "forechoice." This explains the otherwise puzzling remark that "the very name is some indication" that choice involves taking one thing before another.

Aristotle's task has been taken up in turn by several modern philosophers concerned with marking out the field of application and the logical nature of the concept of the voluntary. G. Ryle has argued that we ask only whether *blameworthy* actions are voluntary or involuntary. [2] J. L. Austin has shown that the question of voluntariness is only one of a wide range of questions which might be asked with a view to excusing a blameworthy action; an action may be performed involuntarily, but also

[1] *Laws* 861, Taylor translation.
[2] Chapter III, *The Concept of Mind*.

unintentionally, inadvertently, and so forth, and each of these terms of excuse is used to call attention to *different* kinds of conditions which predominate at different stages of action. Austin also notes that the proper antonym of "voluntary" is not "involuntary," but "constrained"— the antonym of "involuntary" being "deliberate." [3]

These analyses indicate that the field of application for the concept of the voluntary may be much narrower than philosophers have thought. H. L. A. Hart has argued that its logical nature may not even be as philosophers have supposed. To understand this, attention must be paid to the concept of action itself. Hart claims that this concept is not *descriptive,* but is rather *ascriptive.* That is, it is used to ascribe responsibility with regard to rules of conduct. Such ascriptions are, in Hart's terminology, *defeasible;* that is, an ascription of responsibility can be defeated on the basis of various defenses or excuses. He also claims, that these defenses are *heterogeneous,* a claim which he considers to be implicit in Aristotle. This heterogeneity is taken by Hart to rule out the possibility that all these defenses function only as *evidence* against the presence of some single psychological precondition for the voluntariness of an action, such as an act of will. Indeed, he goes on to say that the *force* of such terms as "voluntary" is *only* to exclude these defenses. If the voluntary is not a descriptive concept, efforts to find the mental faculty or event which invests actions with a "quality of voluntariness" must be logically misguided.[4]

What is the bearing of this line of analysis on the philosophical problem of free will? Is that problem based merely on a misinterpretation of the logic of such terms as "action" and "voluntary"? The essay by Hart which follows presents the criticisms of what might be called the mentalistic theory of the voluntary, and also a *rationale* for defenses and excuses, heterogeneous though these may be. This rationale is expressed thus: "What is crucial is that those whom we punish should have, when they acted, the normal capacities, physical and mental, for doing what the law requires and abstaining from what it forbids, and a fair opportunity to exercise those capacities." The evidence that is relevant here is "not different from the evidence we have to use whenever we say of anybody . . . 'He could not have done it' or 'He could have done it.' " We are thus brought full circle to the analysis of the attribution of *abilities* to persons, the question as to the meaning of "can." And this topic remains central to the free will question regardless of any mentalistic theory of volition and the voluntary.

While the problem to which Hart's essay is addressed is set forth clearly in the essay itself, the reader may be perplexed by the phrases *"mens rea"* and "strict liability." The phrase *"mens rea"* can be translated as "crimi-

---

[3] "A Plea for Excuses."
[4] "The Ascription of Responsibility and Rights."

nal intent," and it plays its role in the doctrine *actus non est reus nisi mens sit rea:* "an act is not criminal unless the intent be criminal as well." "Strict liability" refers to the practice of creating liability where there has been no fault, a practice which Hart characterizes as odious, but which is sometimes defended on the ground of social justice, placing loss where it can best be borne. It should be noted that the Austin mentioned in Hart's essay is the jurist, not the philosopher mentioned above.

From *Ethica Eudemia*

ARISTOTLE

Let us, then, take another starting-point for the succeding inquiry. Every substance is by nature a sort of principle; therefore each can produce many similar to itself, as man man, animals in general animals, and plants plants. But in addition to this *man* alone of animals is also the source of certain actions; for no other animal would be said to act. Such principles, which are primary sources of movements, are called principles in the strict sense, and most properly such as have necessary results; God is doubtless a principle of this kind. The strict sense of "principle" is not to be found among principles without movement, e.g. those of mathematics, though by analogy we use the name there also. For there, too, if the principle should change, practically all that is proved from it would alter; but its consequences do not change themselves, one being destroyed by another, except by destroying the assumption and, by its refutation, proving the truth. But man is the source of a kind of movement, for action is movement. But since, as elsewhere, the source or principle is the cause of all that exists or arises through it, we must take the same view as in demonstrations. For if, supposing the triangle to have its angles to two right angles, the quadrilateral must have them equal to four right angles, it is clear that the property of the triangle is the cause of this last. And if the triangle should change, then so must the quadrilateral, having six right angles if the traingle has three, and eight if it has four: but if the former does not change but remains as it was before, so must the quadrilateral.

The necessity of what we are endeavouring to show is clear from the Analytics; at present we can neither affirm nor deny anything with precision except just this.

Supposing there were no further cause for the triangle's having the above property, then the triangle would be a sort of principle or cause of all that comes later. So that if anything existent may have the opposite to its actual qualities, so of necessity may its principles. For what results

From *Ethica Eudemia*, Book II, Chaps. vi-x, translated into English under the editorship of W. D. Ross (Oxford: The Clarendon Press, 1915). Copyright 1925 by The Clarendon Press. Reprinted by permission.

from the necessary is necessary; but the results of the contingent might be the opposite of what they are; what depends on men themselves forms a great portion of contingent matters, and men themselves are the sources of such contingent results. So that it is clear that all the acts of which man is the principle and controller may either happen or not happen, and that their happening or not happening—those at least of whose existence or non-existence he has the control—depends on him. But of what it depends on him to do or not to do, he is himself the cause; and what he is the cause of depends on him. And since virtue and vice and the acts that spring from them are respectively praised or blamed—for we do not praise or blame for what is due to necessity, or chance, or nature, but only for what we ourselves are causes of; for what another is the cause of, for that he bears the blame or praise—it is clear that virtue and vice have to do with matters where the man himself is the cause and source of his acts. We must then ascertain of what actions he is himself the source and cause. Now, we all admit that of acts that are voluntary and done from the deliberate choice of each man he is the cause, but of involuntary acts he is not himself the cause; and all that he does from deliberate choice he clearly does voluntarily. It is clear then that virtue and vice have to do with voluntary acts.

We must then ascertain what is the voluntary and the involuntary, and what is deliberate choice, since by these virtue and vice are defined. First we must consider the voluntary and involuntary. Of three things it would seem to be one: agreement with either desire, or choice, or thought—that is, the voluntary would agree, the involuntary would be contrary to one of these. But again, desire is divided into three sorts, wish, anger, and sensual appetite. We have, then, to distinguish these, and first to consider the case of agreement with sensual appetite.

Now all that is in agreement with sensual appetite would seem to be voluntary; for all the involuntary seems to be forced, and what is forced is painful, and so is all that men do and suffer from compulsion— as Evenus says, "all to which we are compelled is unpleasant." So that if an act is painful it is forced on us, and if forced it is painful. But all that is contrary to sensual appetite is painful—for such appetite is for the pleasant—and therefore forced and involuntary; what then agrees with sensual appetite is voluntary; for these two are opposites. Further, all wickedness makes one more unjust, and incontinence seems to be wicked- ness, the incontinent being the sort of man that acts in accordance with his appetite and contrary to his reason, and shows his incontinence when he acts in accordance with his appetite; but to act unjustly is voluntary, so that the incontinent will act unjustly by acting according to his ap- petite; he will then act voluntarily, and what is done according to appetite is voluntary. Indeed, it would be absurd that those who become incontinent should be more just.

From these considerations, then, the act done from appetite would seem voluntary, but from the following the opposite: what a man does voluntarily he wishes, and what he wishes to do he does voluntarily. But no one wishes what he thinks to be bad; but surely the man who acts incontinently does not do what he wishes, for to act incontinently is to act through appetite contrary to what the man thinks best; whence it results that the same man acts at the same time both voluntarily and involuntarily; but this is impossible. Further, the continent will do a just act, and more so than incontinence; for continence is a virtue, and virtue makes men more just. Now one acts continently whenever he acts against his appetite in accordance with his reason. So that if to act justly is voluntary as to act unjustly is—for both these seem to be voluntary, and if the one is, so must the other be—but action contrary to appetite is involuntary, then the same man will at the same time do the same thing voluntarily and involuntarily.

The same argument may be applied to anger; for there is thought to be a continence and incontinence of anger just as there is of appetite; and what is contrary to our anger is painful, and the repression is forced, so that if the forced is involuntary, all acts done out of anger would be voluntary. Heraclitus, too, seems to be regarding the strength of anger when he says that the restraint of it is painful—"It is hard," he says, "to fight with anger; for it gives its life for what it desires." But if it is impossible for a man voluntarily and involuntarily to do the same thing at the same time, and in regard to the same part of the act, then what is done from wish is more voluntary than that which is done from appetite or anger; and a proof of this is that we do many things voluntarily without anger or desire.

It remains then to consider whether to act from wish and to act voluntarily are identical. But this too seems impossible. For we assumed and all admit that wickedness makes men more unjust, and incontinence seems a kind of wickedness. But the opposite will result from the hypothesis above; for no one wishes what he thinks bad, but does it when he becomes incontinent. If, then, to commit injustice is voluntary, and the voluntary is what agrees with wish, then when a man becomes incontinent he will be no longer committing injustice, but will be more just than before he became incontinent. But this is impossible. That the voluntary then is not action in accordance with desire, nor the involuntary action in opposition to it, is clear.

But again, that action in accordance with, or in opposition to, choice is not the true description of the voluntary and involuntary is clear from the following considerations: it has been shown that the act in agreement with wish was not involuntary, but rather that all that one wishes is voluntary, though it has also been shown that one may do voluntarily what one does not wish. But we do many things from wish suddenly, but no one deliberately chooses an act suddenly.

But if, as we saw, the voluntary must be one of these three—action according either to desire, choice, or thought, and it is not two of these, the remaining alternative is that the voluntary consists in action with some kind of thought. Advancing a little further, let us close our delimitation of the voluntary and the involuntary. To act on compulsion or not on compulsion seems connected with these terms; for we say that the enforced is involuntary, and all the involuntary is enforced: so that first we must consider the action done on compulsion, its nature and its relation to the voluntary and the involuntary. Now the enforced and the necessary, force and necessity, seem opposed to the voluntary and to persuasion in the case of acts done. Generally, we speak of enforced action and necessity even in the case of inanimate things; for we say that a stone moves upwards and fire downwards on compulsion and by force; but when they move according to their natural internal tendency we do not call the act one due to force; nor do we call it voluntary either; there is no name for this antithesis; but when they move contrary to this tendency, then we say they move by force. So, too, among things living and among animals we often see things suffering and acting from force, when something from without moves them contrary to their own internal tendency. Now in the inanimate the moving principle is simple, but in the animated there is more than one principle; for desire and reason do not always agree. And so with the other animals the action on compulsion is simple (just as in the inanimate), for they have not desire and reason opposing one another, but live by desire; but man has both, that is at a certain age, to which we attribute also the power of action; for we do not use this term of the child, nor of the brute, but only of the man who has come to act from reason.

So the compulsory act seems always painful, and no one acts from force and yet with pleasure. Hence there arises much dispute about the continent and incontinent, for each of them acts with two tendencies mutually opposed, so that (as the expression goes) the continent forcibly drags himself from the pleasant appetites (for he feels pain in dragging himself away against the resistance of desire), while the incontinent forcibly drags himself contrary to his reason. But still the latter seems less to be in pain; for appetite is for the pleasant, and this he follows with delight; so that the incontinent rather acts voluntarily and not from force, because he acts without pain. But persuasion is opposed to force and necessity, and the continent goes towards what he is persuaded of, and so proceeds not from force but voluntarily. But appetite leads without persuading, being devoid of reason. We have, then, shown that these alone seem to act from force and involuntarily, and why they seem to, viz. from a certain likeness to the enforced action, in virtue of which we attribute enforced action also to the inanimate. Yet if we add the addition made in our definition, there also the statement becomes untrue. For it is only when something *external* moves a thing, or brings it to rest against its own internal .tendency, that we say this happens by force; otherwise we do not say that it happens by force. But in the continent and the incontinent it is the present *internal* tendency that leads them, for they have both tendencies. So that neither acts on compulsion nor by force, but, as far at least as the above goes, voluntarily. For the external moving principle, that hinders or moves in opposition to the internal tendency, is what we call necessity, e.g. when we strike some one with the hand of one whose wish and appetite alike resist; but when the principle is from within, there is no force. Further, there is both pleasure and pain in both; for the continent feels pain now in acting against his appetite, but has the pleasure of hope, i. e. that he will be presently benefited, or even the pleasure of being actually at present benefited because he is in health; while the incontinent is pleased at getting through his incontinency what he desires, but has a pain of expectation, thinking that he is doing ill. So that to say that both act from compulsion is not without reason, the one sometimes acting involuntarily owing to his desire, the other owing to his reason; these two, being separated, are thrust out by one another. Whence men apply the language to the soul as a whole, because we see something like the above in the case of the elements of the soul. Now of the parts of the soul this may be said; but the soul as a whole, whether in the continent or the incontinent, acts voluntarily, and neither acts on compulsion, but one of the elements in them does, since by nature we have both. For reason is in them by nature, because if growth is permitted and not maimed, it will be there; and appetite, because it accompanies and is present in us from birth. But these are practically the two marks by which we define the natural—it is either that which is found with us as soon as we are born, or that which comes to us if growth is allowed to proceed regularly, e.g. grey hair, old age, and so on. So that either acts, in a way, contrary to nature, and yet, broadly speaking, according to nature, but not the same nature. The puzzles then about the continent and incontinent are these— do both, or one of them, act on compulsion, so that they act involuntarily or else at the same time both on compulsion and voluntarily; that is, if the compulsory is involuntary, both voluntarily and involuntarily? And it is tolerably clear from the above how these puzzles are to be met.

In another way, too, men are said to act by force and compulsion without any disagreement between reason and desire in them, viz. when they do what they consider both painful and bad, but they are threatened with stripes, imprisonment, or death, if they do not do it. Such acts they say they did on compulsion. Or shall we deny this, and say that all do the act itself voluntarily? for they had the power to abstain from doing it, and to submit to the suffering. Again perhaps one might say that some such acts were voluntary and some not. For whatever of the acts that a man does without wishing them he has the power to do or abstain from doing, these he always does voluntarily and not by force; but those in which he has not this power, he does by force in a sense (but not absolutely), because he does not choose the very thing he does, but the purpose for, which it is done, since there is a difference, too, in this. For if a man were to murder another that he might not catch him at blindman's buff he would be laughed at if he were to say that he acted by force, and on compulsion; there ought to be some greater and more painful evil that he would suffer if he did not commit the murder. For then he will act on compulsion, and either by force, or at least not by nature, when he does something evil for the sake of good, or release from a greater evil; then he will at least act involuntarily, for such acts are not subject to his control. Hence, many regard love, anger in some cases, and natural conditions, as involuntary, as being too strong for nature; we feel indulgence for them as things capable of overpowering nature. A man would more seem to act from force and involuntarily, if he acted to escape violent than if to escape gentle pain, and generally if to escape pain than if to get pleasure. For that which depends on him—and all turns on this —is what his nature is able to bear; what it is not, what is not under the control of his natural desire or reason, that does not depend on him. Therefore those who are inspired and prophesy, though their act is one of thought, we still say have it not in their own power either to say what they said, or to do what they did. And so of acts done through appetite. So that some thoughts and passions do not depend on us, nor the acts following such thoughts and reasonings, but, as Philolaus said, some arguments are too strong for us.

So that if the voluntary and involuntary had to be considered in reference to the presence of force as well as from other points of view, let this be our final distinction. Nothing obscures the idea of the voluntary so much as the use of the expression that men act from force and yet voluntarily.

Since we have finished this subject, and we have found the voluntary not to be defined either by desire or by choice, it remains to define it as that which depends on thought. The voluntary, then, seems opposed to the involuntary, and to act with knowledge of the person acted on, instrument and tendency—for sometimes one knows the object, e.g. as father, but not that the tendency of the act is to kill, not to save, as in the case of Pelias's daughters; or knows the object to be a drink but takes it to be a philtre or wine when it was really hemlock—seems opposed to action in ignorance of the person, instrument, or thing, if, that is, the action is essentially the effect of ignorance. All that is done owing to ignorance, whether of person, instrument, or thing, is involuntary; the opposite therefore is voluntary. All, then, that a man does—it being in his power to abstain from doing it—not in ignorance and owing to himself must needs be voluntary; voluntariness is this. But all that he does in ignorance and owing to his ignorance, he does involuntarily. But since science or knowledge is of two sorts, one the possession, the other the use of knowledge, the man who has, but does not use knowledge may in a sense be justly called ignorant, but in another sense not justly, e.g. if he had not used his knowledge owing to carelessness. Similarly, one might be blamed for not having the knowledge, if it were something easy or necessary and he does not have it because of carelessness or pleasure or pain. This, then, we must add to our definition.

Such, then, is the completion of our distinction of the voluntary and the involuntary.

Let us next speak about choice, first raising various difficulties about it. For one might doubt to what genus it belongs and in which to place it, and whether the voluntary and the chosen are or are not the same. Now some insist that choice is either opinion or desire, and the inquirer might well think that it was one or the other, for both are found accompanying it. Now that it is not desire is plain; for then it would be either wish, appetite, or anger, for none desires without having experienced one of these feelings. But anger and appetite belong also to the brutes while choice does not; further, even those who are capable of both the former often choose without either anger or appetite; and when they are under the influence of those passions they do not choose but remain unmoved by them. Further, anger and appetite always involve pain, but we often choose without pain. But neither are wish and choice the same; for we often wish for what we know is impossible, e.g. to rule all mankind or to be immortal, but no one chooses such things unless ignorant of the impossibility, nor even what is possible, generally, if he does not think it in his power to do or to abstain from doing it. So that this is clear, that the object of choice must be one of the things in our own power. Similarly, choice is not an opinion nor, generally, what one thinks; for the object of choice was something in one's power and many things may be thought that are not, e.g. that the diagonal is commensurable; and further, choice is not either true or false. Nor yet is choice identical with our opinion about matters of practice which are in our own power, as when we think that we ought to do or not to do something. This argument applies to wish as well as to opinion; for no one chooses an end, but the means to an end, e.g. no one chooses to be in health, but to walk or to sit for the purpose of keeping well; no one chooses to be happy but to make money or run risks for the purpose of being happy. And in general, in choosing we show both what we choose and for what we choose it, the latter being that for which we choose something else, the former that which we choose for something else. But it is the end that we specially *wish for,* and we *think* we ought to be healthy and happy. So that it is clear through this that choice is different both from opinion and from wish; for wish and opinion are specially of the end, but choice is not.

It is clear, then, that choice is not wish, or opinion, or judgement simply. But in what does it differ from these? How is it related to the voluntary? The answer to these questions will also make it clear what choice is. Of possible things, then, there are some such that we can deliberate about them, while about others we cannot. For some things are possible, but the production of them is not in our power, some being due to nature, others to other causes; and about these none would attempt to deliberate except in ignorance. But about others, not only existence and nonexistence is possible, but also human deliberation; these are things the doing or not doing of which is in our own power. Therefore, we do not deliberate about the affairs of the Indians nor how the circle may be squared; for the first are not in *our* power, the second is wholly beyond the power of action; but we do not even deliberate about all things that may be done and that are in our power (by which it is clear that choice is not opinion simply), though the matters of choice and action belong to the class of things in our own power. One might then raise the problem—why do doctors deliberate about matters within their science, but not grammarians? The reason is that error may occur in two ways (either in reasoning or in perception when we are engaged in the very act), and in medicine one may go wrong in both ways, but in grammar one can do so only in respect of the perception and action, and if they inquired about this there would be no end to their inquiries. Since then choice is neither opinion nor wish singly nor yet both (for no one chooses suddenly, though he thinks he ought to act, and wishes, suddenly), it must be compounded of both, for both are found in a man choosing. But we must ask—how compounded out of these? The very name is some indication. For choice is not simply taking but taking one thing before another; and this is impossible without consideration and deliberation; therefore choice arises out of deliberate opinion.

Now about the end no one deliberates (this being fixed for all), but about that which tends to it—whether this or that tends to it, and—supposing this or that resolved on—how it is to be brought about. All consider this till they have brought the commencement of the production to a point in their own power. If then, no one deliberately chooses without some preparation, without some consideration whether it is better or worse to do so and so, and if one considers all that are in one's power of the means to the end which are capable of existing or not existing, it is clear that choice is a considered desire for something in one's own power; for we all consider what we choose, but we do not choose all that we consider. I call it considered when consideration is the source and cause of the desire, and the man desires because of the consideration. Therefore in the other animals choice does not exist, nor in man at every age or in every condition; for there is not consideration or judgment of the ground of an act; but it is quite possible that many animals have an opinion whether a thing is to be done or not; only thinking with consideration is impossible to them. For the considering part of the soul is that which observes a cause of some sort; and the object of an action is one of the causes; for we call cause that owing to which a thing comes about; but the purpose of a thing's existence or production is what we specially call its cause, e.g. of walking, the fetching of things, if this is the purpose for which one walks. Therefore, those who have no aim fixed have no inclination to deliberate. So that since, if a man of himself and not through ignorance does or abstains from that which is in his power to do or abstain from, he acts or abstains voluntarily, but we do many such things without deliberation or premeditation, it follows that all that has been deliberately chosen is voluntary, but not all the voluntary is deliberately chosen, and that all that is according to choice is voluntary, but not all that is voluntary is according to choice. And at the same time it is clear from this that those legislators define well who enact that some states of feeling are to be considered voluntary, some involuntary, and some premeditated; for if they are not thoroughly accurate, at least they approximate to the truth. But about this we will speak on our investigation of justice; meanwhile, it is clear that deliberate choice is not simply wish or simply opinion, but opinion and desire together when following as a conclusion from deliberation.

But since in deliberating one always deliberates for the sake of some end, and he who deliberates has always an aim by reference to which he judges what is expedient, no one deliberates about the end; this is the starting-point and assumption, like the assumptions in theoretical science (we have spoken about this shortly in the beginning of this work and minutely in the Analytics). Every one's inquiry, whether made with or without art, is about what tends to the end, e.g. whether they shall go to war or not, when this is what they are deliberating about. But the cause or object will come first, e.g. wealth, pleasure, or anything else of the sort that happens to be our object. For the man deliberating deliberates if he has considered, from the point of view of the end, what conduces to bringing the end within his own action, or what he at present can do towards the object. But the object or end is always something good by nature, and men deliberate about its partial constituents, e.g. the doctor whether he is to give a drug, or the general where he is to pitch his camp. To them the absolutely best end is good. But contrary to nature and by perversion not the good but the apparent good is the end. And the reason is that some things cannot be used for anything but what their nature determines, e.g. sight; for one can see nothing but what is

visible, nor hear anything but what is audible. But science enables us
to do what does not belong to that science; for the same science is not
similarly related to health and disease, but naturally to the former, contrary to nature to the latter. And similarly wish is of the good naturally,
but of the bad contrary to nature, and by nature one wishes the good,
but contrary to nature and through perversion the bad as well.

But further, the corruption and perversion of a thing does not tend
to anything at random but to the contrary or the intermediate between
it and the contrary. For out of this province one cannot go, since error
leads not to anything at random but to the contrary of truth where there
is a contrary, and to that contrary which is according to the appropriate
science contrary. Therefore, the error and the resulting choice must de-
viate from the mean towards the opposite—and the opposite of the mean
is excess or defect. And the cause is pleasantness or painfulness; for we
are so constituted that the pleasant appears good to the soul and the
more pleasant better, while the painful appears bad and the more painful
worse. So that from this also it is clear that virtue and vice have to do
with pleasures and pains; for they have to do with objects of choice, and
choice has to do with the good and bad or what seems such, and pleasure
and pain naturally seem such.

It follows then, since moral virtue is itself a mean and wholly con-
concerned with pleasures and pains, and vice lies in excess or defect and is
concerned with the same matters as virtue, that moral virtue is a habit
tending to choose the mean in relation to us in things pleasant and painful, in regard to which, according as one is pleased or pained, men are
said to have a definite sort of character; for one is not said to have a
special sort of character merely for liking what is sweet or what is bitter.

Negligence, Mens Rea and Criminal Responsibility

H. L. A. HART

"I didn't *mean* to do it: I just didn't think." "But you should have thought." Such an exchange, perhaps over the fragments of a broken vase destroyed by some careless action, is not uncommon; and most people would think that, in ordinary circumstances, such a rejection of "I didn't think" as an excuse is quite justified. No doubt many of us have our moments of scepticism about both the justice and the efficacy of the whole business of blaming and punishment; but, if we are going in for the business at all, it does not appear unduly harsh, or a sign of archaic or unenlightened conceptions of responsibility, to include gross, unthinking carelessness among the things for which we blame and punish. This does not seem like the "strict liability" which has acquired such odium among Anglo-American lawyers. There seems a world of difference between punishing people for the harm they unintentionally but carelessly cause, and punishing them for the harm which no exercise of reasonable care on their part could have avoided.

So "I just didn't think" is not in ordinary life, in ordinary circumstances, an excuse; nonetheless it has its place in the rough assessments which we make, outside the law, of the gravity of different offences which cause the same harm. To break your Ming china, deliberately or intentionally, is worse than to knock it over while waltzing wildly round the room and not thinking of what might get knocked over. Hence, showing that the damage was not intentional, but the upshot of thoughtlessness or carelessness, has its relevance as a mitigating factor affecting the quantum of blame or punishment.

THE CRIMINAL LAW

These rough discriminations of ordinary life are worked out with more precision in the criminal law, and most modern writers would agree with

From "Negligence, *Mens Rea,* and Criminal Responsibility," from *Oxford Essays in Jurisprudence,* edited by A. G. Guest (New York: Oxford University Press, 1961). Copyright 1961 by Oxford University Press. Reprinted by permission.

the following distinctions and terminology. "Inadvertent negligence" is to be discriminated not only from deliberately and intentionally doing harm but also from "recklessness," that is, wittingly flying in the face of a substantial, unjustified risk, or the conscious creation of such a risk. The force of the word "inadvertent" is to emphasize the exclusion both of the intention to do harm and the appreciation of the risk; most writers, after stressing this point, then use "negligence" simply for inadvertent negligence.[1] Further, within the sphere of inadvertent negligence, different degrees are discriminated: "gross negligence" is usually said to be required for criminal liability in contrast with something less ("ordinary" or "civil" negligence) which is enough for civil liability.

In Anglo-American law there are a number of statutory offences in which negligence, in the sense of a failure to take reasonable precautions against harm, unaccompanied either by intention to do harm or an appreciation of the risk of harm, is made punishable. In England, the Road Traffic Act, 1930, affords the best known illustration: under section 12 driving without due care and attention is a summary offence even though no harm ensues. In other jurisdictions, criminal codes often contain quite general provisions penalizing those who "negligently hurt" or cause bodily harm by negligence.[2] *Pace* one English authority, Dr. Turner (whose views are examined in detail below), the Common Law as distinct from statute also admits a few crimes,[3] including manslaughter, which can be committed by inadvertent negligence if the negligence is sufficiently "gross." [4] It is, however, the case that a number of English and American

---

[1] This terminology is used by Glanville Williams, *Criminal Law*, ch. 3, p. 82 *et seq.*, and also by the American Law Institute Draft Model Penal Code s. 2.0.2 (Tentative Draft, p. 12 and Comment *ibid.*, pp. 126-127). So, too, Cross and Jones who also use "criminal negligence" to include both "recklessness" and gross inadvertent negligence (*Introduction to Criminal Law* (4th ed.), pp. 47, 48).

[2] See for these and other cases Glanville Williams, *op. cit.*, pp. 97-98, n. 13.

[3] Other common law crimes commonly cited are non-repair of a highway and public nuisance. Besides these there are more important controversial cases including certain forms of murder (*R.* v. *Ward* [1956], 1 Q.B. 351) Cross and Jones, *op. cit.*, 48-52.

[4] See Cross and Jones, *op. cit.*, pp. 145-149. The American Law Institute accepts this view of the English law of manslaughter (Tentative Draft 9, p. 50) but advocates treatment of negligent homicide as an offence of lower degree than manslaughter. Glanville Williams, *op. cit.*, p. 88 (s. 29) after stating that manslaughter "can be committed by inadvertent negligence for the accused need not have foreseen the likelihood of *"death"* says that the "ordinary formulations" leave in doubt the question whether foresight of some bodily harm (not necessarily serious injury or death) is required for manslaughter. He describes as "not altogether satisfactory" the cases usually taken to establish that no such foresight is required viz. *Burdee* (1916), 86 L.J.K.B. 871, 12 Cr. App. Rep. 153; *Pittwood* (1902), 19 T.L.R. 37; *Benge* (1865), 4 F. & F. 504; *John Jones* (1874), 12 Cox 628. Of *Bateman* (1925), 28 Cox 33; 19 Cr. App. Rep. 8 he says "it may be questioned whether [this] does not extend the law of manslaughter too widely" and thinks in spite of *Andrews* v. *D.P.P.*, [1937] A.C. 583 that the issue is still open for the House of Lords.

writers on criminal law feel uneasy about different aspects of negligence. Dr. Glanville Williams[5] thinks that its punishment cannot be justified either on a retributive or a deterrent basis. Professor Jerome Hall[6] who thinks that moral culpability is the basis of criminal responsibility and punishment should be confined to "intentional or reckless doing of a morally wrong act," disputes both the efficacy and justice of the punishment of negligence.

In this essay I shall consider a far more thoroughgoing form of scepticism. It is to be found in Dr. Turner's famous essay *The Mental Element in Crimes at Common Law*.[7] There he makes three claims: first, that negligence has no place in the Common Law as a basis of criminal responsibility, and so none in the law of manslaughter; secondly, that the idea of degrees of negligence and so of gross negligence is nonsensical; thirdly (and most important), that to detach criminal responsibility from what he terms "foresight of consequences," in order to admit negligence as a sufficient basis of such responsibility is necessarily to revert to a system of "absolute" or strict liability in which no "subjective element" is required.

Dr. Turner's essay has of course been very influential: he has reaffirmed the substance of its doctrines in his editions both of Kenny[8] and Russell.[9] This, however, is not my reason for submitting his essay to a fresh scrutiny so long after its publication. My reason is that his arguments have a general interest and importance quite independent of his conclusions about the place of negligence in the Common Law. I shall argue that they rest on a mistaken conception both of the way in which mental or "subjective" elements are involved in human action, and of the reasons why we attach the great importance which we do to the principle that liability to criminal punishment should be conditional on the presence of a mental element. These misconceptions have not been sufficiently examined: yet they are I think widely shared and much encouraged by our traditional legal ways of talking about the relevance of the mind to responsibility. Dr. Turner's arguments are singularly clear and uncompromising; even if I am right in thinking them mistaken his mistakes are illuminating ones. So much cannot always be said for the truths uttered by other men.

Before we reach the substance of the matter one tiresome question of nomenclature must be got out of the way. This concerns the meaning of

[5] *Op. cit.*, pp. 98-99.

[6] *Principles of Criminal Law*, pp. 149, 166, 167, 245. Professor Herbert Wechsler (Reporter in the A.L.I. Draft Model Penal Code) rejects this criticism and holds that punishment for conduct which inadvertently creates improper risks "supplies men with additional motives to take care before acting to use their faculties and to draw on their experience in gauging the potentialities of contemplated conduct." Tentative Draft 4, p. 126.

[7] *The Modern Approach to Criminal Law* (1945), p. 195.

[8] Kenny's *Outlines of Criminal Law* (17th ed.), pp. 33-35, 172-174.

[9] *Russell on Crime* (11th ed.), pp. 46-47, 53-56, 60-66.

the phrase "*mens rea.*" Dr. Turner, as we shall see, confines this expression to a combination of two elements, one of which is the element required if the accused's conduct is to be "voluntary," the other is "foresight" of the consequences of conduct. Dr. Glanville Williams, although he deprecates the imposition of criminal punishment for negligence, does not describe it or (apparently) think of it, as Dr. Turner does, as a form of "strict" or "absolute" liability; nonetheless, though not including it under the expression "strict liability," he excludes it from the scope of the term "*mens rea,*" which he confines to intention and recklessness. Judicial pronouncements, though no very careful ones, can be cited on either side.[10]

There is, I think, much to be said in mid-twentieth century in favor of extending the notion of "*mens*" beyond the "cognitive" element of knowledge or foresight, so as to include the capacities and powers of normal persons to think about and control their conduct: I would therefore certainly follow Stephen and others and include negligence in "*mens rea*" because, as I argue later, it is essentially a culpable failure to exercise such capacities. But this question of nomenclature is not important so long as it is seen for what it is, and not allowed either to obscure or prejudge the issue of substance. For the substantial issue is not whether negligence should be *called* "*mens rea*"; the issue is whether it is true that to admit negligence as a basis of criminal responsibility is *eo ipso* to eliminate from the conditions of criminal responsibility the subjective element which, according to modern conceptions of justice, the law should require. Is its admission tantamount to that "strict" liability which we now generally hold odious and tolerate with reluctance?

VOLUNTARY CONDUCT AND FORESIGHT OF CONSEQUENCES

According to Dr. Turner, the subjective element required for responsibility for common law crimes consists of two distinct items specified in the second and third of three general rules which he formulates:

Rule I—It must be proved that the conduct of the accused person caused the *actus reus.*

Rule II—It must be proved that this conduct was *voluntary.*

Rule III—It must be proved that the accused person *realised at the time* that his conduct would, or might *produce results of a certain kind,* in other

[10] See Glanville Williams, *op. cit.*, p. 87, n. 12. Examples on each side are Shearman J. in *Allard* v. *Selfridge* [1925], 1 K.B. 129, at p. 137. "The true translation of that phrase is criminal intention or an intention to do the act which is made penal by statute or common law" and Fry, L.J. in *Lee* v. *Dangar, Grant & Co.* [1892], 2 Q.B. 337, at p. 350. "A criminal mind or that negligence which is itself criminal." See also for a more discursive statement *R.* v. *Bateman* (1925), 19 Cr. App. Rep. 8 or 133 L.T. 730 *per* Hewart, L.C.J.

words that he must have foreseen that certain consequences were likely to follow on his acts or omissions. The extent to which this foresight of consequences must have extended is fixed by law and differs in the case of each specific crime. . . .[11]

We shall be mainly concerned with Rule III—as is Dr. Turner's essay. But something must be said about the stipulation in Rule II that the accused's "conduct" must be "voluntary." Dr. Turner himself considers that the truth contained in his Rule III has been obscured because the mental element required to make conduct voluntary has not been discriminated as a separate item in *mens rea*. I, on the other hand, harbor the suspicion that a failure on Dr. Turner's part to explore properly what is involved in the notion of "voluntary conduct" is responsible for much that seems to me mistaken in his further argument.

Certainly it is not easy to extract either from this essay or from Dr. Turner's editions of Kenny or Russell what is meant by "conduct," and what the mental element is which makes conduct "voluntary." At first sight Dr. Turner's doctrine on this matter looks very like the old simple Austinian[12] theory that what we normally speak of and think of as actions (killing, hitting, etc.) must be divided into two parts (*a*) the "act" or initiating movement of the actor's body or (in more extreme versions) a muscular contraction, (*b*) the consequences of the "act"; so that an "act" is voluntary when and only when it is caused by a "volition" which is a desire for the movement (or muscular contraction). But such an identification of Dr. Turner's "conduct" with the Austinian "act" (or movement of the body), and the mental element which makes it voluntary with the Austinian volition or desire for movement, is precluded by two things. First, Dr. Turner says conduct includes not only physical acts but omissions. Secondly, though "conduct" is always something less than the *actus reus* which is its "result" (e.g. killing in murder) it is by no means confined by him as "act" is by Austin to the mere initiating movement of the actor's body. Dr. Turner tells us that "by definition *conduct, as such, cannot be criminal.*"[13] He also explains that "conduct is of course itself a series of deeds, each of which is the result of those which have come before it; but at some stage in this series a position of affairs may be brought into existence which the governing power in the state regards as so harmful as to call for repression by the criminal law. It is this point of selection by the law, this designation of an event as an *actus reus*, which for the purposes of our jurisprudence marks the distinction between *conduct* and *deed*.[14]

---

[11] *The Modern Approach to Criminal Law* (1945), p. 199.
[12] Austin, *Lectures on Jurisprudence* (5th ed.) Lecture XVIII.
[13] *Op. cit.*, p. 240.
[14] *Op. cit.*, p. 239.

About the mental element required to make conduct voluntary, Dr. Turner tells us[15] only that it is a "mental attitude to [his] conduct" (as distinct from the consequences of conduct) and that if conduct is to be voluntary "it is essential that the conduct should have been the result of the exercise of the will." He does however give us examples of involuntary conduct in a list not meant to be exhaustive, "for example, if *B* holds a weapon and *A*, against *B*'s will seizes his hand, and the weapon and therewith stabs *C*; and possibly an act done under hypnotic suggestion or when sleep-walking or by pure accident. In certain cases of insanity, infancy and drunkenness the same defence may be successfully raised."[16]

This account of voluntary conduct presents many difficulties. What is it for conduct to be "the result of the exercise of the will"? Must the actor desire or will only the initiating movement of his body or the whole course of "conduct" short of the point when it becomes an *actus reus*? And how does this account apply to omissions, as Dr. Turner asserts it does? How can we draw in the case of omissions the distinction between the course of conduct and the *actus reus* which is said to be its "result"? The examples given suggest that Dr. Turner is here grossly hampered by traces of the old psychology of "act" and "volition," and no satisfactory account of what it is which makes "conduct" voluntary or involuntary, capable of covering both acts and omissions can be given in his terminology of "states of mind," or "mental attitude." What is required (as a minimum) is the notion of a general *ability* or *capacity* to control bodily movements, which is usually present but may be absent or impaired.

But even if we waive these difficulties, Dr. Turner's twofold account of *mens rea* in terms of "voluntary conduct" and "foresight of consequences" is at points plainly inadequate. It does not fit certain quite straightforward, familiar cases where criminal responsibility is excluded because of the lack of the appropriate subjective element. Thus it does not, as it stands, accommodate the case of mistake; for a mistaken belief sufficient to exclude liability need not necessarily relate to *consequences*; it may relate to *circumstances* in which the action is done, or to the character or identity of the thing or person affected. Of course, Dr. Turner in his edition of Kenny under the title of "Mistake as a Defence at Common Law" discusses well-known cases of mistake such as *Levett's case*,[17] where the innocent victim was killed in mistake for a burglar, and says (in a footnote) that the subjective element in such cases relates to the agent's "knowledge of the facts upon which he takes action."[18] He does

---

[15] Kenny (17th ed.), p. 27.
[16] *The Modern Approach to Criminal Law* (1945), p. 204. See the further examples suggested in Kenny (17th ed.), p. 26-27: *viz.*, when harm "results from a man's movements in an epileptic seizure or while suffering from St. Vitus's Dance."
[17] (1638), Cro. Car. 538.
[18] *Op. cit.*, (17th ed.), p. 53.

not think this calls for a modification in his two-limbed general theory of *mens rea*; instead he adopts the view that such mistakes, since they do not relate to consequences, negative an element in the *actus reus* but do not negative *mens rea*. Besides this curious treatment of mistake, there is also the group of defences which Dr. Turner discusses in the same work under the heading of Compulsion,[19] which include marital coercion and duress *per minas*. Here, as the author rightly says, English law is "both meagre and vague"; nonetheless, confidence in his general definition as an exhaustive account of *mens rea* has led him into a curious explanation of the theoretical basis of the relevance to responsibility of such matters as coercion or duress. He cites first as a simple example of compulsion the case of "a powerful man who, seizing the hand of one much weaker than himself and overcoming his resistance by sheer strength, forces the hand to strike someone else."[20] Of this case he says, "the defense . . . must be that the mental element of "volition" is absent. The accused, in other words, pleads that his conduct was not voluntary"[21] and to explain this he refers back to the earlier account of voluntary conduct which we have discussed. The author then says that compulsion can take other forms than physical force,[22] and he proceeds to discuss under this head obedience to orders, marital coercion, duress, and necessity. It is, however, clear that such defences as coercion or duress (where they are admitted) lie quite outside the ambit of the definition of voluntary *conduct* given by Dr. Turner: they are not just different instances of *movement* which is not voluntary because, like the case of physical compulsion or that of epilepsy cited earlier, the agent has no control over his bodily movements. Defenses like duress or coercion refer not to involuntary *movements*, but, as Austin[23] himself emphasized, to other, quite different ways in which an *action* may fail to be voluntary; here the *action* may not be the outcome of the agent's free choice, though the *movements* of the body are not in any way involuntary.

So far, my objection is that Dr. Turner's formulation of the subjective element in terms of the two elements of voluntary conduct and foresight of consequences leads to a mis-assimilation of different cases; as if the difference between an action under duress and involuntary *conduct* lay merely in the kind of compulsion used. But in fact the definition of *mens rea* in terms of voluntary conduct *plus* foresight of consequences, leads Dr. Turner to great incoherence in the division of the ingredients of a crime between *mens rea and actus reus*. Thus in discussing the wellknown

[19] *Ibid.*, p. 61.
[20] *Ibid.*
[21] *Ibid.*
[22] *Ibid.*
[23] *Op. cit.*, p. 417. Notes to Lecture, XVIII, "Voluntary—Double Meaning of the word Voluntary."

case of *R.* v. *Prince*[24] (where the accused was found guilty of the statutory
offence of taking a girl under 16 out of the possession of her father
notwithstanding that he believed on reasonable grounds that she was
over 16) Dr. Turner examines[25] the argument that the word "knowingly"
might have been read into the section creating the offense (in which case
the offense would not have been committed by the prisoner) and says
"this change would not affect the *mens rea* of the accused person, but it
would merely add another necessary fact to the *actus reus,* namely the
offender's knowledge of the girl's age." But there is nothing to support [26]
this startling view that where knowledge is required as an ingredient of
an offense this may be part of the *actus reus,* not of the *mens rea,* except
the author's definition of *mens rea* exclusively in terms of the two elements
of "voluntary conduct" and "foresight of consequences." If knowledge
(the constituent *par excellence* of *mens rea*) may be counted as part of
the *actus reus,* it seems quite senseless to insist on any distinction at all
between the *actus reus* and the *mens rea,* or to develop a doctrine of
criminal responsibility in terms of this distinction.

NEGLIGENCE AND INADVERTENCE

So far it is plain that, quite apart from its exclusion of negligence, the
account of the subjective element required for criminal responsibility in
terms of the two elements "voluntary conduct" and "foresight of consequences" is, at certain points, inadequate. Dr. Turner's arguments
against the inclusion of negligence must now be examined. They are
most clearly presented by him in connection with manslaughter. Of this,
Dr. Turner says[27] "a man, to be guilty of manslaughter, must have had in
his mind the idea of bodily harm to someone." On this view, what is
known to English law as "manslaughter by negligence" is misdescribed
by the words; and Dr. Turner expressly says that judges in trying cases
of manslaughter should avoid all reference to "negligence" and so far as
mens rea is concerned should direct the jury to two questions:
(1)   Whether the accused's conduct was voluntary;
(2)   Whether at the time he either intended to inflict on someone physical
      harm, or foresaw the possibility of inflicting a physical harm and
      took the risk of it.[28]

[24] (1875), L.R. 2 C.C.R. 154.
[25] In "The Mental Element in Crimes at Common Law": *The Modern Approach
to Criminal Law* (1945), p. 219.
[26] There is plain authority against it: see *R.* v. *Tolson* (1889), 23 Q.B.D. 168 *per*
Stephen J. "The mental element of most crimes is marked by one of the words 'mali-
cious,' 'fraudulently,' 'negligently,' or 'knowingly.'"
[27] *The Modern Approach to Criminal Law* (1945), p. 228.
[28] *Ibid.,* p. 231.

To treat these cases otherwise would, it is suggested, be to eliminate the element of *mens rea* as an element in criminal liability and to return to the old rule of strict or absolute liability.

In developing his argument Dr. Turner roundly asserts that negligence is a state of mind. It is "the state of mind of a man who pursues a course of conduct without adverting at all to the consequences."[29] Dr. Turner admits that this state of mind may be "blameworthy"[30] and ground *civil* liability. Here it is important to pause and note that if anything is "blameworthy," it is not the "state of mind" but the agent's failure to inform himself of the facts and so *getting into* this "state of mind." But, says Dr. Turner, "Negligence in its proper meaning of inadvertence cannot at Common Law amount to *mens rea*,"[31] for "no one could reasonably contend that a man, in a fit of inadvertence, could make himself guilty of the following crimes, arson, burglary, rape, robbery . . ."[32] This of course is quite true; but proves nothing at all, until it is independently shown that to act negligently is the same as to act in "a fit of inadvertence." Precisely the same comment applies to the use made by Dr. Turner of many cases[33] where the judges have insisted that for criminal responsibility "mere inadvertence" is not enough.

It is of course most important at this point to realize that the issue here is *not* merely a verbal one which the dictionary might settle. Much more is at stake; for Dr. Turner is really attempting by the use of his definitions to establish his general doctrine that if a man is to be held criminally responsible he must "have in his mind the idea of bodily harm to someone," by suggesting that the only alternative to this is the quite repugnant doctrine that a man may be criminally liable for mere inadvertence when, through no failure of his to which the criminal law could attach importance, his mind is a mere blank. This alternative indeed would threaten to eliminate the doctrine of *mens rea*. But we must not be stampeded into the belief that we are faced with this dilemma. For there are not just two alternatives; we can perfectly well both deny that a man may be criminally responsible for "mere inadvertence" and also deny that he is only responsible if "he has an idea of harm in his mind to someone." Thus, to take the familiar example, a workman who is mending a roof in a busy town starts to throw down into the street building materials without first bothering to take the elementary precaution of looking to see that no one is passing at the time. We are surely not forced to choose, as Dr. Turner's argument suggests, between

[29] *Ibid.*, p. 207.
[30] *Ibid.*, p. 208.
[31] *Ibid.*, p. 209.
[32] *Ibid.*
[33] E.g., *R.* v. *Finney* (1874), 12 Cox 625. See also *R.* v. *Bateman, Andrews,* v. *D.P.P.,* and others discussed *op. cit.*, pp. 216-217.

two alternatives: (1) Did he have the idea of harm in his mind? (2) Did he merely act in a fit of inadvertence? Why should we not say that he has been grossly negligent because he has failed, though not deliberately, to take the most elementary of the precautions that the law requires him to take in order to avoid harm to others?

At this point, a careful consideration is needed of the differences between the meaning of expressions like "inadvertently" and "while his mind was a blank" on the one hand, and "negligently" on the other. In ordinary English, and also in lawyers' English, when harm has resulted from someone's negligence, if we say of that person that he has acted negligently we are not thereby *merely* describing the frame of mind in which he acted. "He negligently broke a saucer" is not the same *kind* of expression as "He inadvertently broke the saucer." The point of the adverb "inadvertently" is merely to inform us of the agent's psychological state, whereas if we say "He broke it negligently" we are not merely adding to this an element of blame or reproach, but something quite specific, *viz.* we are referring to the fact that the agent failed to comply with a standard of conduct with which any ordinary reasonable man *could* and *would* have complied: a standard requiring him to take precautions against harm. The word "negligently," both in legal and in non-legal contexts, makes an essential reference to an omission to do what is thus required: it is not a flatly descriptive psychological expression like "his mind was a blank."

By contrast, if we say of an agent "He acted inadvertently," this contains no implications that the agent fell below any standard of conduct. Indeed it is most often proffered as an excuse. "X hit Smith inadvertently" means that X, in the course of doing some other action, (*e.g.* sweeping the floor) through failing to attend to his bodily movements (*e.g.* his attention being distracted) and *a fortiori* not foreseeing the consequences, hit Smith.

There is of course a *connection*, and an important one, between inadvertence and negligence, and it is this. Very often if we are to comply with a rule or standard requiring us to take precautions against harm we must, before we act, acquire certain information: we must examine or *advert* to the situation and its possible dangers (e.g. see if the gun we are playing with is loaded) and watch our bodily movements (handle the gun carefully if it is loaded). But this connection far from identifying the concepts of negligence and inadvertence shows them to be different. *Through* our negligence in not examining the situation before acting or in attending to it as we act, we may fail to realise the possibly harmful consequences of what we are doing and as to these our mind is in a sense a "blank"; but the negligence does not, of course, consist in this blank state of mind but in our failure to take precautions against harm by examining the situation. Crudely put, "negligence" is not the name of "a state of mind" while "inadvertence" is.

We must now confront the claim made by Dr. Turner that there is an absurdity in stipulating that a special (gross) degree of negligence is required. "There can be no different degree of inadvertence as indicating a state of mind. The man's mind is a blank as to the consequences; his realization of their possibility is nothing and there are no different degrees of nothing." [34] This *reductio ad absurdum* of the notion of gross negligence depends entirely on the view that negligence is merely a name for a state of mind consisting in the absence of foresight of consequences. Surely we should require something more to persuade us to drop notions so firmly embedded, not only in the law, but in common speech, as "very negligent," "gross carelessness," a "minor form of negligence." Negligence is gross if the precautions to be taken against harm are very simple, such as persons who are but poorly endowed with physical and mental capacities can easily take.[35] So, in the workman's case, it was gross negligence not to look and see before throwing off the slates; perhaps it was somewhat less gross (because it required more exertion and thought) to have failed to shout a warning for those not yet in view; it was less gross still to have failed to have put up some warning notice in the street below.

NEGLIGENCE AND NORMAL CAPACITIES

At the root of Dr. Turner's arguments there lie, I think, certain unexamined assumptions as to what the mind is and why its "states" are relevant to responsibility. Dr. Turner obviously thinks that unless a man "has in his mind the idea of harm to someone" it is not only bad law, but morally objectionable as a recourse to strict or absolute liability, to punish him. But here we should ask why, in or out of law courts, we should attach this crucial importance to foresight of consequences, to the "having of an idea in the mind of harm to someone." On what theory of responsibility is it that the presence of this particular item of mental furniture is taken to be something which makes it perfectly satisfactory to hold that the agent is responsible for what he did? And why should we necessarily conclude that in its absence an agent cannot be decently held responsible? I suspect, in Dr. Turner's doctrine, a form of the ancient belief that possession of knowledge of consequences is a necessary and sufficient condition of the capacity for self-control, so that if the agent knows the consequences of his action we are bound to say "he could have helped it"; and, by parity of reasoning, if he does not know the consequences of his action, even though he failed to examine or think about the situation before acting, we are bound to say that he could not have helped it.

[34] *Op. cit.*, p. 211.
[35] "It is such a degree of negligence as excludes the loosest degree of care" *per* Hewart C.J. in *R. v. Bateman* (1925), 133 L.T. 730.

Neither of these views are acceptable. The first is not only incompatible with what large numbers of scientists and lawyers and plain men now believe about the capacity of human beings for self-control. But it is also true that there is nothing to compel us to say "He could not have helped it" in *all* cases where a man omits to think about or examine the situation in which he acts and harm results which he has not foreseen. Sometimes we do say this and should say it; this is so when we have evidence, from the personal history of the agent or other sources, that his memory or other faculties were defective, or that he could not distinguish a dangerous situation from a harmless one, or where we know that repeated instructions and punishment have been of no avail. From such evidence we may conclude that he was unable to attend to, or examine the situation, or to assess its risks; often we find this so in the case of a child or a lunatic. We should wish to distinguish from such cases the case of a signalman whose duty it is to signal a train if the evidence clearly shows that he has the normal capacities of memory and observation and intelligence. He may say after the disaster, "Yes, I went off to play a game of cards. I just didn't stop to think about the 10.15 when I was asked to play." Why, in such a case, should we say "He could not help it—because his mind was a blank as to the consequences"? The kind of evidence we have to go upon in distinguishing those omissions to attend to, or examine, or think about the situation and assess its risks before acting which we treat as culpable, from those omissions (*e.g.* on the part of infants or mentally deficient persons) for which we do not hold the agent responsible, is not different from the evidence we have to use whenever we say of anybody who has failed to do something "He could not have done it" or "He could have done it." The evidence in such cases relates to the general capacities of the agent; it is drawn, not only from the facts of the instant case, but from many sources, such as his previous behavior, the known effect upon him of instruction or punishment, etc. Only a theory that mental operations like attending to, or thinking about, or examining a situation are somehow "either there or not there," and so utterly outside our control, can lead to the theory that we are *never* responsible if, like the signalman who forgets to pull the signal, we fail to think or remember. And this theory of the uncontrollable character of mental operations would, of course, be fatal to responsibility for even the most cold-blooded, deliberate action performed by an agent with the maximum "foresight." For just as the signalman, inspired by Dr. Turner's argument, might say "My mind was a blank" or "I just forgot" or "I just didn't think, I could not help not thinking" so the cold-blooded murderer might say "I just decided to kill; I couldn't help deciding." In the latter case we do not normally allow this plea because we know from the general history of the agent, and others like him, that he could have acted differently. This general evidence is what is relevant to the question of responsibility, not the mere presence or absence of foresight. We should have doubts, which now find legal expression in the category of diminished responsibility, even in the case of deliberate murder, if it were shown that in spite of every warning and every danger and without a comprehensible motive the agent had deliberately and repeatedly planned and committed murder. After all, a hundred times a day persons are blamed outside the law courts for not being more careful, for being inattentive and not stopping to think; in particular cases, their history or mental or physical examination may show that they could not have done what they omitted to do. In such cases they are not responsible; but if anyone is ever responsible for anything, there is no general reason why men should not be responsible for such omissions to think, or to consider the situation and its dangers before acting.

SUBJECTIVE AND OBJECTIVE

Excessive distrust of negligence and excessive confidence in the respectability of "foresight of harm" or "having the thought of harm on the mind" as a ground of responsibility have their roots in a common misunderstanding. Both oversimplify the character of the subjective element required in those whom we punish if it is to be morally tolerable according to common notions of justice to punish them. The reason why, according to modern ideas, strict liability is odious, and appears as a sacrifice of a valued principle which we should make, if at all, only for some over-riding social good, is not merely because it amounts, as it does, to punishing those who did not at the time of acting "have in their minds" the elements of foresight or desire for muscular movement. These psychological elements are not *in themselves* crucial though they are important as aspects of responsibility. What is crucial is that those whom we punish should have, when they acted, the normal capacities, physical and mental, for doing what the law requires and abstaining from what it forbids, and a fair opportunity to exercise these capacities. Where these are absent as they are in different ways in the varied cases of accident, mistake, paralysis, reflex action, coercion, insanity, etc., the moral protest is that it is morally wrong to punish because "he could not have helped it" or "he could have done otherwise" or "he had no real choice." But, as we have seen, there is no reason (unless we are to reject the whole business of responsibility and punishment) *always* to make this protest when someone who "just didn't think" is punished for carelessness. For in some cases at least we may say "he could have thought about what he was doing" with just as much rational confidence as one can say of any intentional wrongdoing "he could have done otherwise."

Of course, the law compromises with competing values over this matter of the subjective element in responsibility as it does over other matters.

All legal systems temper their respect for the principle that persons should not be punished if they could not have done otherwise *i.e.*, had neither the capacity nor a fair opportunity to act otherwise. Sometimes this is done in deference to genuine practical difficulties of proof; sometimes it represents an obstinate refusal to recognise that human beings may not be able to control their conduct though they know what they are doing. Difficulties of proof may lead one system to limit consideration of the subjective element to the question whether a person acted intentionally and had volitional control of his muscular movements; other systems may let the inquiry go further and, in relation to some offences, consider whether the accused had, owing to some external cause, lost the power of such control, or whether his capacity to control was "diminished" by mental abnormality or disease. In these last cases exemplified in "provocation" and "diminished responsibility," if we punish at all we punish *less,* on the footing that, though the accused's capacity to self-control was not absent, its exercise was a matter of abnormal difficulty. He is punished in effect for a *culpable* loss of control; and this too is involved when punishment for negligence is morally justifiable.

The most important compromise which legal systems make over the subjective element consists in its adoption of what has been unhappily termed the "objective standard." This may lead to an individual being treated for the purposes of conviction and punishment as if he possessed capacities for control of his conduct which he did not possess, but which an ordinary or reasonable man possesses and would have exercised. The expression "objective" and its partner "subjective" are unhappy because, as far as negligence is concerned, they obscure the real issue. We may be tempted to say with Dr. Turner that just because the negligent man does not have "the thought of harm in his mind," to hold him responsible for negligence is necessarily to adopt an objective standard and to abandon the "subjective" element in responsibility. It then becomes vital to distinguish this (mistaken) thesis from the position brought about by the use of objective standards in the application of laws which make negligence criminally punishable. For, when negligence is made criminally punishable, this itself leaves open the question: whether, before we punish, both or only the first of the following two questions must be answered affirmatively:

(1) Did the accused fail to take those precautions which any reasonable man with normal capacities would in the circumstances have taken?
(2) Could the accused, given his mental and physical capacities, have taken those precautions?

One use of the dangerous expressions "objective" and "subjective" is to make the distinction between these two questions; given the ambiguities of those expressions, this distinction would have been more happily expressed by the expressions "invariant" standard of care, and "individ-uated conditions of liability." It may well be that, even if the "standard of care" is pitched very low so that individuals are held liable only if they fail to take very elementary precautions against harm, there will still be some unfortunate individuals who, through lack of intelligence, powers of concentration, memory, or clumsiness, could not attain even this low standard. If our conditions of liability are invariant and not flexible, *i.e.* if they are not adjusted to the capacities of the accused, then some individuals will be held liable for negligence though they could not have helped their failure to comply with the standard. In *such* cases, indeed, criminal responsibility will be made independent of any "subjec-tive element": since the accused could not have conformed to the required standard. But this result is nothing to do with negligence being taken as a basis of criminal liability; precisely the same result will be reached if, in considering whether a person acted intentionally, we were to attribute to him foresight of consequences which a reasonable man would have foreseen but he did not. "Absolute liability" results not from the admission of the principle that one who has been grossly negligent is criminally responsible for the harm that results even if "he had no idea in his mind of harm to anyone," but from the refusal in the application of this principle to consider the capacities of an individual who has fal-len below the standard of care.

It is of course quite arguably that no legal system could afford to individuate the conditions of liability so far as to discover and excuse all those who could not attain the average or reasonable man's standard. It may, in practice, be impossible to do more than excuse those who suffer from gross forms of incapacity, *viz.* infants, or the insane, or those afflicted with recognizably inadequate powers of control over their move-ments, or who are clearly unable to detect or extricate themselves from situations in which their disability may work harm. Some confusion is, however, engendered by certain inappropriate ways of describing these excusable cases which we are tempted to use in a system which, like our own, defines negligence in terms of what the reasonable man would do. We may find ourselves asking whether the infant, the insane, or those suffering from paralysis did all that a reasonable man would *in the cir-cumstances* do, taking "circumstances" (most queerly) to include personal qualities like being an infant, insane or paralysed. This paradoxical ap-proach leads to many difficulties. To avoid them we need to hold apart the primary question (1) What *would* the reasonable man with ordinary capacities have done in these circumstances? from the second question (2), *Could* the accused with *his* capacities have done that? Reference to such factors as lunacy or disease should be made in answering only the second of these questions. This simple, and surely realistic, approach avoids difficulties which the notion of individualizing the standard of care has presented for certain writers; for these difficulties are usually created by the mistaken assumption that the only way of allowing for individual incapacities is to treat them as part of the "circumstances" in which the reasonable man is supposed to be acting. Thus Dr. Glanville Williams says that if "regard must be had to the make-up and circumstances of the particular offender, one would seem on a determinist view of conduct to be pushed to the conclusion that there is no standard of conduct at all. For if every characteristic of the individual is taken into account, including his heredity the conclusion is that he could not help doing what he did." [36]

But "determinism" presents no special difficulty here. The question is whether the individual had the capacity (inherited or not) to act otherwise than he did, and "determinism" has no relevance to the case of one who is accused of negligence which it does not have to one accused of intentionally killing. Dr. Williams supports his arguments by discussion of the case of a motorist whom a blow or illness has rendered incapable of driving properly. His conclusion, tentatively expressed, is that if the blow or illness occurred long ago or in infancy he should not be excused, but if it occurred shortly before the driving in respect of which he is charged he should. Only thus, it seems to him, can any standard of conduct be preserved. But there seems no need to make this extraordinary distinction. Again, the first question which we should ask is: What *would* a reasonable driver with normal capacities have done? The second question is whether or not the accused driver had at the time he drove the normal capacity of control (either in the actual conduct of the vehicle in driving or in the decision to engage in driving). If he was incapable, the date recent or otherwise of the causal origin of the incapacity is surely beside the point, except that if it was of long standing, this would suggest that he knew of it and was neglectful in driving with that knowledge.

Equally obscure to me are the reasons given by Dr. Williams for doubting the efficacy of punishment for negligence. He asks, "Even if a person admits that he occasionally makes a negligent mistake, how, in the nature of things, can punishment for inadvertence serve to deter?" [37] But if this question is meant as an argument, it rests on the old, mistaken identification of the "subjective element" involved in negligence with "a blank mind," whereas it is in fact a failure to exercise the capacity to advert to, and to think about and control, conduct and its risks. Surely we have plenty of empirical evidence to show, as Professor Wechsler has said, that "punishment may stimulate persons to make a better use of the faculties which they have in the past failed to exercise." Again there is no difficulty here peculiar to negligence, though of course we can doubt the efficacy of any punishment to deter any kind of offence.

[36] *Op. cit.*, p. 82.
[37] *Op. cit.*, p. 92.

I should add (out of abundant caution) that I have not been concerned here to advocate punishing negligence, though, perhaps, better acquaintance with motoring offences would convert me into a passionate advocate. My concern has been to show only that the belief that criminal responsibility for negligence is a form of strict or absolute liability, rests on a confused conception of the "subjective element" and its relation to responsibility.

BIBLIOGRAPHY

This is a selected bibliography. Comprehensive bibliographies can be found on pages 623-63 of M. Adler, *The Idea of Freedom* (Garden City, New York: Doubleday & Co., Inc., 1958), and pages 529-47 of H. Morris, ed., *Freedom and Responsibility* (Stanford: Stanford University Press, 1961). Where possible, we have cited inexpensive editions.

Alexander, A., *Theories of the Will in the History of Philosophy*. New York: Charles Scribner's Sons, 1898.

Anscombe, G. E. M., *Intention*. Oxford: Basil Blackwell, 1957.

Aquinas, St. Thomas, *Basic Writings of Saint Thomas Aquinas*, edited and annotated, with an introduction by A. C. Pegis. New York: Random House, 1945.

————, *Truth*, translated by R. W. Mulligan, J. V. McGlynn, R. W. Schmidt. Chicago: Henry Regnery Co., 1952-1954.

Aristotle, *The Eudemian Ethics*, translated by J. Solomon. "The Works of Aristotle," Vol. IX, W. D. Ross, ed. New York: Oxford University Press, 1940.

————, *The Nicomachean Ethics*, translated by J. A. K. Thomson. Harmondsworth: Penguin Books Ltd., 1955.

Augustine, St., *Augustine: Earlier Writings*, selected and translated with introductions by J. H. S. Burleigh. "The Library of Christian Classics," Vol. VI. Philadelphia: The Westminster Press, 1953.

————, *Basic Writings of Saint Augustine*, edited with introduction and notes by W. J. Oates. New York: Random House, 1948.

————, *Augustine: Later Works*, selected and translated with introductions by J. Burnaby. "The Library of Christian Classics," Vol. VIII. Philadelphia: The Westminster Press, 1955.

Austin, J. L., "A Plea for Excuses," *Proceedings of the Aristotelian Society*, LVII (1956-1957), pp. 1-30.

————, "Ifs and Cans," *Proceedings of the British Academy*, 42 (1956), pp. 109-132.

Ayer, A. J., "Freedom and Necessity," reprinted in *Philosophical Essays*. London: Macmillan & Co., Ltd., 1954.

Bergson, Henri, *Time and Free Will,* translated by F. L. Pogson. London: George Allen & Unwin, 1950.

Berlin, I., *Historical Inevitability.* London: Oxford University Press, 1954.

Boring, E. G., "When is Human Behavior Predetermined?" reprinted in D. E. Dulany, ed., *Contributions to Modern Psychology.* New York: Oxford University Press, 1958.

Bradley, F. H., "The Vulgar Notion of Responsibility in Connection with the Theories of Free-Will and Necessity," in *Ethical Studies.* Oxford: Clarendon Press, 1927.

Bradley, R. D., "Free Will: Problem or Pseudo-problem?" *Australasian Journal of Philosophy,* XXXVI (1958), pp. 33-45.

Broad, C. D., "Determinism, Indeterminism, and Libertarianism," in *Ethics and the History of Philosophy.* London: Routledge & Kegan Paul Ltd., 1952.

Campbell, C. A., "Free Will: A Reply to Mr. R. D. Bradley," *Australasian Journal of Philosophy,* XXXVI (1958), pp. 46-56.

————, "In Defense of Free-Will." Glasgow: Jackson, Sons, and Co., 1938. Reprinted in M. Munitz, ed., *A Modern Introduction to Ethics.* Glencoe, Illinois: The Free Press, 1958.

————, "Is 'Free-Will' a Pseudo-Problem?" *Mind,* LX (1951), pp. 441-465. Reprinted in P. Edwards and A. Pap, eds., *A Modern Introduction to Philosophy.* Glencoe, Illinois: The Free Press, 1957.

————, *On Self-Hood and God-Hood.* London: George Allen & Unwin, 1957.

————, *Scepticism and Construction.* London: George Allen & Unwin, 1931.

Danto, A. and Morgenbesser, S., "Character and Free Will," *The Journal of Philosophy,* LIV (1957), pp. 493-505.

Descartes, R., "Of the True and the False," Meditation IV, *Meditations on First Philosophy,* translated with an introduction by L. J. Lafleur. New York: The Liberal Arts Press, 1951.

Ebersole, F. B., "Free-Choice and the Demands of Morals," *Mind,* LXI (1952), pp. 234-257.

Edwards, Jonathan, *Freedom of the Will,* ed. P. Ramsey. New Haven: Yale University Press, 1957.

Erasmus, D. and Luther, M., *Discourse on Free Will* (two treatises), edited and translated by E. Winter. New York: F. Ungar Publishing Co., 1961.

Ewing, A. C., "Indeterminism," *The Review of Metaphysics,* V (1951), pp. 199-222.

Farrer, A., *The Freedom of the Will.* New York: Charles Scribner's Sons, 1958

Foot, P., "Free Will as Involving Determinism," *The Philosophical Review,* LXVI (1957), pp. 439-450.

Gilson, E., "Free-Will and Christian Liberty," Chapter XV, *The Spirit of Medieval Philosophy,* translated by A. H. C. Downes. London: Sheed & Ward, 1936.

Hampshire, S., *Thought and Action.* London: Chatto and Windus, 1959.

————, Maclagan, W. G., and R. M. Hare, "The Freedom of the Will," a symposium in *Proceedings of the Aristotelian Society*, Supplementary Volume XXV (1951), pp. 161-216.

Hart, H. L. A., "The Ascription of Responsibility and Rights," in *Logic and Language*, First Series, edited by A. G. N. Flew. Oxford: Basil Blackwell, 1952.

———, "Negligence, *Mens Rea* and Criminal Responsibility," in *Oxford Essays in Jurisprudence*, edited by A. G. Guest. Oxford: Oxford University Press, 1961.

Hartmann, N., "Moral Freedom," in *Ethics*, Vol. III, translated by S. Coit. New York: The Macmillan Co., 1932.

Herbst, P., "Freedom and Prediction," *Mind*, LXVI (1957), pp. 1-27.

Hobart, R. B., "Free-Will as Involving Determinism and Inconceivable Without It," *Mind*, LXIII (1934), pp. 1-27.

Hobbes, T., "Of the Liberty of Subjects," *Leviathan*, Chapter XXI. New York: The Liberal Arts Press, 1958.

———, *The Questions Concerning Liberty, Necessity, and Chance*, Vol. V of *The English Works of Thomas Hobbes*, edited by Sir William Molesworth, Bart. London: John Bohn, 1841.

Hook, S., ed., *Determinism and Freedom*. New York: Collier Books, 1961.

Hospers, J., "Free-Will and Psychoanalysis," in W. Sellars and J. Hospers, eds., *Readings in Ethical Theory*. New York: Appleton-Century-Crofts, 1952.

Hume, D., "Of Liberty and Necessity," *An Inquiry Concerning Human Understanding*, Section VIII, edited by C. W. Hendel. New York: The Liberal Arts Press, 1955.

———, "Of the Will and Direct Passions," *A Treatise of Human Nature*, Book II, Part III. Garden City, N. Y.: Doubleday & Co., Inc., 1961.

James, W., "The Dilemma of Determinism," in *The Will to Believe*. New York: Longmans, Green, and Co., 1921. Reprinted by Dover Publications, Inc. Reprinted in P. Edwards and A. Pap, eds., *A Modern Introduction to Philosophy*. Glencoe, Illinois: The Free Press, 1957.

Kant, I., *Critique of Practical Reason*, translated by L. W. Beck. Chicago: Chicago University Press, 1949.

———, "Transcendental Dialectic," *Critique of Pure Reason*, Chapter II, Book II, translated by N. Kemp-Smith. New York: The Modern Library, 1958.

———, *Foundations of the Metaphysics of Morals*, translated by L. W. Beck. New York: The Liberal Arts Press, 1959.

———, *Religion Within the Limits of Reason Alone*, translated by T. M. Greene and H. H. Hudson. New York: Harper Torchbooks, 1960.

Ladd, J., "Free Will and Voluntary Action," *Philosophy and Phenomenological Research*, LII (1952), pp. 392-405.

Laird, J., *On Human Freedom*. London: George Allen and Unwin Ltd., 1947.

Lewis, H. D., "Guilt and Freedom," *Proceedings of the Aristotelian Society*, Supplementary Volume XXI. Reprinted in M. Munitz, ed., *A Modern Introduction to Ethics*. Glencoe, Illinois: The Free Press, 1958.

———, "Moral Freedom in Recent Ethics," *Proceedings of the Aristotelian Society*, XLVII (1946-1947), pp. 1-26.

Locke, J., "Of the Idea of Power," *An Essay Concerning Human Understanding,* Book II, Chapter XXI. London: J. M. Dent & Sons Ltd., 1947.

MacIntyre, A., "Determinism," *Mind,* LXVI (1957), pp. 28-41.

Matson, W. I., "On the Irrelevance of Free-will to Moral Responsibility and the Vacuity of the Latter," *Mind,* LXV (1956), pp. 489-497.

Melden, A. I., *Free Action.* London: Routledge and Kegan Paul, 1961.

Mill, J. S., "On the Freedom of the Will," *An Examination of Sir William Hamilton's Philosophy,* Chapter XXVI. London: Longmans, Green, Reader and Dyer, 1867.

———, "Of Liberty and Necessity," *A System of Logic,* Book VI, Chapter 2. New York: Harper & Brothers, Publishers, 1873.

Moore, G. E., "Free Will," *Ethics,* Chapter VI. London: Oxford University Press, 1912.

Nowell-Smith, P. H., "Determinists and Libertarians," *Mind,* LXII (1954), pp. 317-337.

———, "Freedom and Responsibility," *Ethics,* Chapters 19 and 20. Harmondsworth: Penguin Books Ltd., 1954.

———, "Freewill and Moral Responsibility," *Mind,* LVII (1948), pp. 45-61. Reprinted in M. Munitz, ed., *A Modern Introduction to Ethics.* Glencoe, Illinois: The Free Press, 1958.

———, "Ifs and Cans," *Theoria,* XXVI (1960), pp. 85-101.

Ofstad, H., *An Inquiry into the Freedom of Decision.* Oslo: Oslo University Press, 1961.

Origen, *De Principiis,* Book III, Chapter I, "On the Freedom of the Will," Vol. IV, "The Ante-Nicene Fathers," translated by Rev. F. Crombie. New York: The Christian Literature Company, 1890.

Palmer, G. H., *The Problem of Freedom.* Boston: Houghton Mifflin Company, 1911.

Peirce, C., "The Doctrine of Necessity Examined," reprinted in J. Buchler, ed., *Philosophical Writings of Peirce.* New York: Dover Publications, 1955.

Peters, R. S., McCraken, D. J., and J. O. Urmson, "Motives and Causes," a symposium in *Proceedings of the Aristotelian Society,* Supplementary Volume XXVI (1952), pp. 139-194.

Plato, *Laws,* Book IX, translated by A. E. Taylor. London: J. M. Dent & Sons Ltd., 1934.

———, *Phaedo,* translated with introduction and commentary by R. Hackforth. Cambridge: Cambridge University Press, 1952.

———, *Protagoras,* translated by B. Jowett, revised by M. Ostwald. New York: The Liberal Arts Press, 1956.

———, *Republic,* translated by H. Lee. Harmondsworth: Penguin Books Ltd., 1955.

Rankin, K., *Choice and Chance.* Oxford: Basil Blackwell, 1961.

Raphael, D. D., "Causation and Free Will," *The Philosophical Quarterly,* II (1952), pp. 13-30.

Rashdall, H., *The Theory of Good and Evil,* Book III, Chapter III. Oxford: Oxford University Press, 1924.

Ross, W. D., "Indeterminacy and Indeterminism," *Foundations of Ethics,* Chapter X. Oxford: Clarendon Press, 1939.

Ryle, G., "It Was to Be," *Dilemmas,* Chapter II. Cambridge: Cambridge University Press, 1954.

———, "The Will," *The Concept of Mind,* Chapter III. New York: Barnes & Noble Inc., 1949.

Sartre, J. P., *Being and Nothingness,* translated with introduction by H. Barnes. New York: The Philosophical Library, 1956.

Schlick, M., *Problems of Ethics,* Chapter VII, translated by D. Rynin. New York: Prentice-Hall, Inc., 1939. Reprinted in P. Edwards and A. Pap, eds., *A Modern Introduction to Philosophy.* Glencoe, Illinois: The Free Press, 1957.

Schopenhauer, A., "Free-Will and Fatalism," in *Complete Essays,* translated by T. Saunders. New York: Willey Book Company, 1942.

Shute, C., "The Dilemma of Determinism after Seventy-five Years," *Mind,* LXX (1961), pp. 331-350.

Sidgwick, H., "Free Will," *The Methods of Ethics,* Book I, Chapter V. London: Macmillan & Co. Ltd., 1877.

Smart, J., "Free-will, Praise and Blame," *Mind,* LXX (1961), pp. 291-306.

Spinoza, B., *Ethics,* edited with introduction by J. Gutmann. New York: Hafner Publishing Company, 1949.

Stevenson, C., "Avoidability; Indeterminism." *Ethics and Language,* Chapter XIV. New Haven: Yale University Press, 1944.

Taube, M., *Causation, Freedom and Determinism* (a discussion of seventeenth-century positions). London: George Allen & Unwin Ltd., 1936.

Taylor, R., "I Can," *The Philosophical Review,* LXIX (1960), pp. 78-89.

———, "The Problem of Future Contingencies," *The Philosophical Review,* LXVI (1957), pp. 1-28.

University of California Associates, "The Freedom of the Will," reprinted in H. Feigl and W. Sellars, eds., *Readings in Philosophical Analysis.* New York: Appleton-Century-Crofts, Inc., 1949.

Wilson, J., "Freedom and Compulsion," *Mind,* LXVII (1958), pp. 60-69.

SPECTRUM PAPERBACKS

OTHER SPECTRUM BOOKS . . . *quality paper-backs that meet the highest standards of scholarship and integrity.*

* Also available in limited clothbound edition.

The American Assembly Series*

Classics in History Series*

* Also available in limited clothbound edition.

Science and Technical Series*

Twentieth Century Views Series*

* Also available in limited clothbound edition.